## DATE DUE

| DATE DUE | | | |
|---|---|---|---|
| NOV 2 9 1982 | | | |
| NOV 2 5 1995 | | | |
| | | | |
| | | | |
| | | | |
| | | | |
| | | | |
| | | | |
| | | | |
| | | | |
| GAYLORD 234 | | | PRINTED IN U. S. A. |

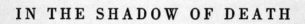

IN THE SHADOW OF DEATH

# IN THE
# SHADOW *of* DEATH

*12090*

## MEDITATIONS
## FOR THE SICK-ROOM AND
## AT THE DEATH-BED
### *by*
### *ABRAHAM KUYPER, D.D., LL.D.*
FORMER PRIME MINISTER OF THE NETHERLANDS

*Though I walk through the valley of*
*the shadow of death, I will fear no evil.*
Ps. 23, 4

TRANSLATED FROM THE DUTCH BY
JOHN HENDRIK DE VRIES, D.D.

---

## WM·B·EERDMANS PUBL·CO
GRAND RAPIDS·MICH·

THAT *the message of strength and comfort, which this volume brings to the sick-room may continue its mission in the new, as it does in its original, dress, is the prayer wherewith the Translator offers it to the English-speaking Christian world.*

*Walpole, Mass., July 28, 1929.*

# CONTENTS

vii

Not yet a *prey* of death; even not yet *appointed* to die; but in such a way, that death casts already its somber shadow upon you.

So it is at the deathbed.

So it is at the beginning in every sick-room.

And therefore against that power of death with every deathbed and in every sick-room the sound of the Prince of Life must go out.

Hence this volume with the title: *In the Valley of the Shadow of Death*. Meditations in the style of what I wrote before in *Honey from the Rock*; in *Days of Glad Tidings*; and others.

What we received as inheritance from former ages for the sick-room and for the deathbed, speaks no longer our language; and however deeply thought out and tender it might be, it has become too labored for many ears. Before they grasp the meaning, the charm for them is lost. So it does not interest; does not carry them along; and tunes, nor supports, nor edifies the hidden man of the heart.

Hence the effort, here put forth, to offer something at least, that as a beginning can meet the existing want. A series of meditations. First, to weep with those who weep, written for others on whose way of life I saw that Death had cast his somber shadow, whether they came out again into the happy light, or traveled the valley to the grave to the end; later, after I myself had wept at the grave of an unforgettable child, completed from experience of my own soul.

May this little volume find an opened ear at many a sick-bed. May it address many a wrestler in that bitter struggle, against which there is no resistance. And also at the dying, and after the departure, of those who are torn away from the heart, may it pour balsam into the wound of those who remained behind.

KUYPER.

AMSTERDAM, *June* 28, 1893.

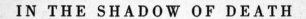

IN THE SHADOW OF DEATH

## *"If Ye Be Without Chastisement"*

### DIVINE CHASTISEMENT

"BASTARD" is a hard word, for use in the church of Christ; and yet it is entirely in place; for "bastard" is the real name for a hypocrite, or, more accurately still, for every one, who chooses the outward, without belonging to the inward church.

The church then appears in the image of the woman, who has God for "her husband," as Scripture tells us of the daughter of Zion. But this woman defiles her paths, runs after her paramours, brings forth an unholy progeny, which grows up in her family, but stands *outside the* childship of God.

These two sorts of children therefore must each have a mark of their own; for the legitimate children obtain the inheritance, which the bastard does not; and it is with an eye to this, that the holy apostle commands you, to seek one of these marks in *chastisement*.

When you see a man engaged in beating a child, not from anger but with calmness, then, ten to one, you know that that man is the *father* of that child; and you are quite sure of this, even when you had never seen that man or that child before; yea, though you were witness to such a scene in an altogether far and foreign land.

The right and duty of that chastisement lies in the nature of *fatherhood*, in connection with the sinful nature, in which every child grows up. And thus in this

1

power of fatherhood as well as in this relation to the sinful child, the father on earth is nothing but a faint shadow-image of the *Father in the heavens*, Whose power over His child is absolute, and over against Whom the child stands in a yet far unholier attitude.

Thus it is entirely natural, that in His church God the Lord chastises all those who stand in His heavenly childship. And when in the church you see persons, whom the Father in heaven passes by, and whom He never chastises, there is justification for the saying: That man or woman can be *no* child of that Father.

And, therefore, says the apostle: "If ye (i.e., in God's church) be without chastisement, whereof all (all children of God) are partakers, then are ye *bastards*, and not *sons*" (Hebr. 12, 8).

How is this meant?

When the apostle speaks of people, who are without chastisement, does he refer to those individual world-lings, of which Asaph sang: "There are no bands in their death, and they are not in trouble like other men"? (Ps. 73, 4, 5).

Surely not.

For then experience should have to teach that God's children alone drink the cup of suffering, and that, from the cradle to the grave, all people of the world walk a path of roses. Which is *not* so. For also among the people of the world there is much bitter complaint and gloomy suffering. To them also it applies: "By thine anger are we consumed" (Ps. 90). And, on the contrary, there are many children of God, who, when you compare them with many a child of the world, have known almost no suffering.

So taken, you would establish an altogether false standard and arrive at an altogether false conclusion. A conclusion, which would lead the converted soul, to invoke suffering, to covet sorrow, and when the cross tarried, to seek it by reckless self-chastisement.

This untrue antithesis therefore must altogether be set aside. There is no mention here of people who do, and people who do not know adversity; but of persons *with*, and persons *without* CHASTISEMENT.

A chastisement is something altogether different from a draught of the cup of suffering. When a man is assaulted by another man on the way and severely beaten by him, it will neither occur to him, nor to any one else, to say, that that man is *chastised*.

Or, when, heated by strong drink, a wicked father comes home, and tries to compel his children to drink, and they refuse to do it, and he strikes them, there will no one call this a fatherly *chastisement*.

*Chastisement* is only then and then alone, when punishment overtakes me at the hand of some one, who has the right of say over me, and my conscience bears witness, that I have deserved it.

AND hereby the apostolic word is become clear to us.

Yet this by no means implies that you are the more certain of your childship, according as you have to bear a more bitter lot on earth. For there have been many miscreants, and many naughty people, who have had to bear a dreadful lot, and who had nothing in common with a child of God.

But from this follows, that a child of God views every frustration of his plans, every stumbling-block in his way, every adversity he has to combat, in brief, everything that makes his happiness to be incomplete, as *not* belonging to his state as child of God, and thus endures it as something that is really foreign to his state.

That he, moreover, views these small and common hindrances as something which people do not do to him, and does not come upon him by chance, but as something that is brought upon him by his Father Who is in heaven, Who indeed was able to spare him this, but evidently deems it profitable and necessary for him to suffer it.

And finally, that seeing, in everything that is lacking or wanting in his perfect happiness, a direct act of his God, he feels himself smitten in his conscience, acknowledges and confesses that by his sin he has deserved it, that to deter him from sin it is necessary for him, and therefore in humble brokenness of heart he kisses the hand that smites him.

Now take a man, who after the world's standard is well-to-do; has ample means to satisfy every desire; enjoys abounding health; has a happy family; occupies an honorable position; who, forsooth, has to get along with these minor bitternesses, disappointments and disagreeablenesses of life, but takes them all as ordinary thorns, which are always part of the branch, on which roses grow; who makes the most of them; and with self-satisfaction even laughs about them; in that case there is every ground to surmise, that in God's family this man is *no* child of the Father in the heavens, but a *bastard*.

For here you have to do with a man who is content with a very limited and small measure of happiness, and therefore seems to have no idea of the glory, that really belongs to a child of God. He evidently is a man who takes these ordinary bitternesses of life as something that comes by accident or Fate or at the hands of men, and who in connection with them has no thought of his heavenly Father. And then you observe in everything, that instead of making it a matter of conscience, and of humbling himself, by reason of all these bitter drops that are mingled in his cup, he lives outside of his soul, and dismisses it all with a haughty smile.

Take, on the other hand, people who make the bold pretense that their happiness really ought to be perfect; who, extremely sensitive as they are, feel day by day that everything troubles them, galls their cup and burdens them on the way; and who yet, far from being morose thereby or dissatisfied, on the contrary, see God's appointment in all this, the doings of their Father in the heavens, and quietly, reverently humble themselves under it all, even to borrow from it a stimulus to live ever more painstakingly; then you observe, that you are *not* dealing with bastards, but with *real* children of your God.

AND if you ask, why then the cross weighs so heavily upon some of God's children, while others, relatively, have so little adversity in life, then the question itself already is ungodly, when it implies a finding fault with God's providential direction.

Little people of six and more years of age, who do not understand why father, sister and mother did as they did, and now together come to the conclusion, that their parents were mistaken, are not children, but little wise-acres.

And how much more then do we make ourselves objects of ridicule, when we, insignificant children of men, would censure the doings full of majesty on the part of the high God.

If on the other hand you put this question, that in the midst of the storms of life you might have a compass, then observe the following:

First, that driving nails into iron demands a firmer blow than driving nails into a wainscot. If then there are two children of God, whose hearts are unequal in hardening, so that one can be compared with iron, the other with the weaker wainscot, then it is altogether natural, that the one must be struck far more forcibly than the other.

Secondly, you well know, that a diamond is far more difficult to cut than a piece of crystal. Upon a diamond ten and twenty times more strength must be expended.

From Jesus' parable you know that not all God's children are alike. Once they shall shine as stars in the firmament, but not all stars are equal in glory.

Hence there is nothing unnatural, but something quite understandable in it, that God cuts His diamonds more sharply than His crystal lenses. Did He not do so, the diamond would never have its brightness glitter.

And thirdly, the surgeon operates externally, in

case of an outward festering or dislocation; but the physician inwardly, when externally everything remained sound, but the corruption is within; and both do this in keeping with the condition of the patient. And so among God's children the case can be, that one is severely affected in his outward lot, and the other almost not at all, and that yet the latter suffers no less, but with a suffering, which you scarcely observe.

## II

## "He Keepeth All His Bones"

### ALSO YOUR BODY IN GOD'S HAND

WHEN the Roman soldiers deemed their task on Golgotha ended, they proceeded to break the legs of the crosslings.

This was so prescribed to them; partly as an act of mercy, in this way to make an end to the nameless sufferings of the crosslings. So they did this only, when in the crucified persons there was still some sign of life; but not, when it was convincingly apparent, that the crossling was already dead.

Yet it was not purely merciful. There also spake in it conceited coarseness. The death of the sentenced persons had to be certified. And cruel wantonness took pleasure in striking with an iron bolt, or anything else that was at hand, the legs of the crosslings, till they were broken. An unholy mockery, as though to make sure, that they would no more be able to run away from the cross.

Now Holy Scripture expressly states, that in the case of the Lord Jesus this breaking of the legs, as superfluous, did not take place. He was already dead, and thus with Him this was not done.

And with respect to this the Evangelist observes, that here was fulfilled a word, that ages ago had been proclaimed by the Psalmist, when he sang: "He keepeth all his bones: not one of them is broken" (Ps. 34, 20).

Something that from the nature of the case does not mean to say, that David foretold this exclusively with an eye to Jesus.

On the contrary, his statement is altogether *general*. They are the "servants of the Lord" (v. 22); "the broken of heart and contrite of spirit" (v. 18); in brief, the righteous, of which he says: "Many are the afflictions of the righteous: but the Lord delivereth him out of them all" (v. 19); and then immediately adds: "He keepeth all his bones; not one of them is broken," without any mention of the Messiah.

But, of course, when the Lord shows such tender care extending even to the hidden skeleton of His servants, in highest measure the same care must come to the good of "the suffering servant of the Lord," i.e., the Messiah; and in that sense only on Golgotha has the full, deep significance of this glorious word been confirmed.

The danger was that with rough violence the body of Jesus would be broken. And this would certainly not have stood in the way of His resurrection.

But yet, it could not be.

Divine solicitude watched against so shocking a maiming of Jesus' body.

And when the soldier passed Jesus by, it was God, Who from on high kept watch over His holy child Jesus.

Thus on that cross He kept all His bones, and not one of them was broken.

And only so is also this Scripture fulfilled in Jesus.

BUT so there lies likewise in this statement, that the Lord keeps all our bones, real comfort.

In Scripture the dissection of our body is by no means scientific anatomy.

What Scripture says regarding it, is reckoned purely after the practical sense, that every one of us has of his own body. Consequently the main distinction is, that we consist of a skeleton, and that this skeleton is clothed with flesh.

In the vision, which Ezekiel had of the valley of dry bones, this is most strongly evident. This distinction also is altogether natural; for when one has died, and his corpse is decomposed, the skeleton, or, if you like, skull and crossbones, is all that remains.

So these bones form the *hidden* part of our body. What we see with the living body is flesh with blood, which shines through in the face. But that flesh has no existence by itself. Flesh is merely the covering of that, wherein consists the real structure of our body; and that structure is our skeleton, as it is called with the dead, or, what with the living may be called, the internal framework of the body.

Bones therefore are the *hidden* part of our body, which we ourselves never see. For the form of it may be apparent underneath skin and flesh; and through skin and muscle one may feel his bones; but, apart from dreadful mutilation, no one has ever seen his own bones.

To our skin, and even to our flesh, to a certain extent we can impart care; but not to our bones.

They have been constructed outside of our knowing; independently of us they are cared for and maintained.

Scripture concerns itself a good deal about *our body*; far more than one would infer from preaching in general. We incline, as soon as we enter the sacred domain, all too readily to lose ourselves solely in the *spiritual*, and leave alone everything that concerns our body. Something that, in ordinary life, usually avenges itself in lack of dominion over the body.

But Scripture does *not* do so.

She comes back every time to *your body* again, to remind you, how wonderfully that body has been wrought by God, when as an embroidery you were woven in your mother's womb. To tell you, that it was God, Who has implanted your ear, and that same God, Who granted you your eye. To point out to you, that it is God the Lord, Who has determined the height of your body, so that you can neither add to nor detract anything from it. And that it is the same God, Who day by day feeds and sustains your body. To declare unto you, that God knows every tear that flows from your eye, and has numbered all the hairs on your head. Yea, that it is the Lord your God Who, in times of pestilence and distress, commands His angels to watch over your body. And Who, when once your body becomes a prey of death, even as a corpse still keeps it in His protection, in order presently, when the day of glory dawns, to restore the same to you in glorified beauty.

And in this sense, Scripture also points you to your hidden frame, and assures you, that to this also extends the protection of God's almightiness.

He keeps not only your body, but in that body also all your bones.

God sees them.

And He it is, Who as the God of our life, also keeps this *hidden* part of our body.

AND this operates upon our inner sense.

God's word always wills that you should think of your God not only in His loftiness and majesty, as He is enthroned high above you in the heavens; but that your God shall also be to you a God near by.

Real piety discovers ever more clearly, that in Him we live, and *move* and have our being.

And you should not thoughtlessly glance at that word *move*, but understand well, that you never move yourself, except as your bones pass over from one position into another.

The apostle therefore wills just what David wills, and urges you to become aware of God's omnipotent power in yourself, and also in your body.

That you shall not think: "Here I live, and yonder far above me *lives God*," but that you shall know, and in your own perception shall be aware, that you yourself live, and move and are in your God, and that it is the power of His life, that inworks and reveals itself in your breathing, in the glow of your blood, and also in the motions, in the feeding, in the resistance-power of your bones.

Also your body is an instrument of the Lord, that surely must serve you, but in the first place must serve Him, to make Himself known to you, and in your own perception of life to make you aware of the working of His almightiness.

Again and again the body leads you away from God. This cannot be otherwise. This is our sin. But this does not take away, that your body just the same retains the calling, of leading you to God. Not only by meditating on God's wonder-working power, that created and maintained you, but much more yet by discovering your God in yourself, as the One, Who also in the hidden part of your body, from moment to moment, inworks with His Divine power.

Only so is the life of your body taken up into the life of your piety, and it will become ever less strange to you, to believe in the resurrection of your body after death.

Even though in death you must let your body drop away, and with your soul separate from it, God does not for this reason abandon it.

He, Who all the days of your life keeps all your bones, also keeps them in sickness and accident. He is that wondrous God, Who, also when your dead bones are given a prey to dissolution, does not cease to preserve you also after the body, and Who shall once gloriously also after your body bring you out again.

## III

# "The Strength of My Life"

## THE STRENGTH OF YOUR LIFE

WHEN some one needed encouragement, when some one needed to be roused or put upon his mettle, the call of the Jews was: "Be strong," or as in the original tongue: *Chazak*.

They did not call out *Achtung*, like the Germans, neither: *Attention*, like the French, nor: *Look out*, like the Dutch.

A man in Israel felt differently from us, and therefore did not think of being on guard, or of paying attention, or of giving heed, but of the *vital strength* that was required.

Be strong; muster your powers; fit yourself to the task, as we might put it. And the art, of making oneself able to meet the requirement, cáme up to the high level of this rule of piety: "Be strong and He shall strengthen thine heart, yea, wait, I say, on the Lord."

So it reads at the end of Psalm 27; and in connection herewith this same song begins with the glorious witness: "The Lord is the *strength of my life*."

Far more than we incline of ourselves, the Scripture binds us to keep count with the strength, with the power, with the might to live and to persevere. "Thou hast strengthened me with strength in my soul" (Ps. 138), is taken as exclamation from the world of Scripture thought. In Psalm 31 it reads likewise: "He shall *strengthen* your heart." Of the Messiah it reads in Psalm 89: "Mine arm also shall *strengthen* him." And with the

14

Old Testament in the lead, like this, the New Testament follows on, for there also we read the prayer: "That he might *strengthen you with might* in the inner man" (Eph. 3, 16).

Thus Scripture is an enemy to slackness. She antagonizes lassitude and barrenness. She makes no peace with emotionalism and speculation.

Her demand is that there be strength in the children of God and that strength shall go out from them, since strength flows out toward us from the Source of all strength and the Fountain of all mightinesses.


"THE Lord is the strength of my life," jubilates the Sionite.

He does not presume, therefore, that he is here merely to think of his understanding and his will, but before all things else, he counts with what lies back of his understanding and his will, that is to say, with his being, with his existence, with his life, and with the power, by which that life originated and is maintained and shall endure.

Superficiality Scripture hates. She goes deep. No, it is not a matter of course, that you are and have life. The very fact that you are and received life and were kept in life, is the first miracle, that must address you. For you it is the miracle closest by. The miracle that touches you personally.

It is not enough, along this line, that you go back to your father and your mother, because your father has generated and your mother has borne you. See it in verse 10: also father and mother die and leave you, but though you are left behind lonesome and desolate, in the root of your life you are not cut off, for that root of your being, whence springs the life-sap of your strength, is your God.

"The strength of my life" is therefore nothing else nor anything less than the direct working of God's almightiness in my own body and in my own soul, and in the combination of both.

Now it may be that you are hale and hearty and strong, that that mightiness of the Lord God potently operates in you, and yet that you are godless, godless because you feel that you yourself are strong, and thus derive that hale and hearty strength of life not from your God, but attribute it to yourself.

You the strong one, if needs be, able to get along without your God, yea, in haughtiness and overboldness at length to place yourself over against your God.

For such is the fierce character of sin in us.

When we feel ourselves weak, and sink in, and observe that the strength of our life wears out and succumbs, then the song: "The Lord is the strength of my life" begins to become dear to us.

But so long as that "strength of life" operates soundly and undisturbedly in us, we take it to be our own strength, and forget the Lord Whose handiwork we are.

EVEN when God's child is spiritually enlightened, it goes frequently so faulty with respect to this.

Then you observe again and again, that he truly thinks of grace received, that he realizes it and feels that without this grace he can for no single moment keep his path straight. But, O, so many have no thought, that before all things else this rule of faith must be applied to their existence, to their being, to the strength whereby they live and are.

The psalmist always begins with the natural. What the apostle teaches, "that the natural is first, after that the spiritual," he puts in practice in every psalm.

He always goes out from the fact of his own life, from his existence as man among men, from his needs and wants, from the dangers that threaten him, from the enemies that lay snares for him, and from the strength that keeps him standing amidst it all; only from the natural to ascend to the spiritual, to the higher, to the eternal.

You can say briefly: In Scripture it always goes out from God's almightiness, and only after that almightiness is confessed and worshiped, it ascends from this to the holiness, the righteousness and the compassions of the Lord.

No onesided counting with the work of the Holy Spirit and the work of the Son, but always back of both the work of the Father in the confession of His almightiness.

Even as in the twelve articles of Faith the church begins, first: "I believe in God the Father, the Almighty," and after that: "I believe in the Holy Ghost."

ONLY so comes unity in the life of God's child.

Not *on one side* an inanimate and deadening life in his body and in his home and in his business, and *alongside of this* a highly attuned life in the soul and in the circle of believers; and these two placed side by side as circles, which do not touch each other.

Such doubleness of life Scripture knows nothing of, and our Reformed confession abhors it.

Both circles must have *one and the selfsame* center, and for both this center must lie in the Lord our God. From Him every outpouring of strength in our daily life; and from that selfsame Covenant-God every outpouring in our spiritual life; and both these outpourings of strength from one and the selfsame source and in one selfsame person, disposed to one another, the one supporting the other, because one selfsame Divine wisdom unites both.

*The Lord is the strength of my life,* is the blessed utterance of soul, which coincides with the *Pray without ceasing.*

For, if you truly live in that sacred consciousness, that, from moment to moment, the strength of your life, by which you live and from which you live, is not in yourself, does not flow toward you from the world, but comes to you from the living God, then every breath, every heart-throb, every pulse-beat is to you a sign from the side of God, that at that very moment He maintains you, carries you by His strength and operates in you.

Your own life in you is then a witness of God's omnipresence and of God's almightiness, and every evening, that you kneel down before Him and lose yourself in the worship of the Eternal, is then to you a receiving anew of your own existence from the hand of your God.

To take food and drink, is then no longer a mere feeding of your blood, as cattle do by eating grass, but a conscious and devout placing yourself under the care of your God, Who, by what is provided on your table, comes to increase the strength of your life; and the blessing which you invoke is then nothing less, than desiring from your God, that by it He will renew and refresh the strength of your life.

Thus devoutness is not, of every sixty minutes in an hour to live fifty-nine without God, and then for a single minute to think of your God, but a constant, steady, continuous resting in the faithfulness, in the majesty and in the almightiness of your God.

If then there come days of trouble, when care and anxiety well-nigh strangle the heart, or sudden danger overtakes you, or the strength for labor falls short, or sickness or the approach of death makes you pine away in yourself, then such a devout practical life in the fellowship of the Lord bears its choicest fruit.

You then went up and down with your God. You became more and more accustomed to Him. Yea, even in your minutest interests and least significant difficulties of life you have then learned to lean upon your God. And that constant practice has given your soul the bent for it, has made it a second nature to you, so that it would be difficult for you to exist otherwise.

The strength of your life is no longer in you, but in the Lord, and now in days of trouble or distress of

soul there comes to you of itself from that rich, deep
conviction of soul the grace of a perfectly sufficing con-
solation.

For if the Lord withdraws His strength from you,
all your anxiety and all your exertion will avail you
nothing. And when He continues to grant you this
strength of life, there is then no power in heaven or on
earth, that can break His might.

Does a difficult task await you, He Who imposed
that task upon you, is Himself the strength of your life,
Who at that very moment from His almightiness shall
pour the strength in you.

And does sickness overtake you, or the hour draw
near when you must die, even then there is nothing gone,
because you lie down in weakness, or presently depart
from the earth.

For He is the strength of your life, and that strength
which maintains you in existence, operates likewise in
and beyond the grave, and *continues* forever in the
heavens.

## IV

# "The Soul of Man Is a Candle of the Lord"

## SOUL AND BODY

SCRIPTURE-LANGUAGE is not rich in names for all the hidden parts of our body.

In the years when the Spirit of the Lord compiled the Holy Scripture, anatomy was not what it is now. When therefore there is mention of "the belly" this must not be understood in an artificial way, but as a general expression for the whole middle-part of your body. Hence, that it is also used for what we call our heart, or nature.

That middle-part of your body the Scripture compares to an house, and in that house she imagines chambers that face the outside, and chambers that face toward inner courts, and because that middle part of your body has no eyes, she presents these inner chambers *as dark*.

But in those dark inner chambers of your body she now tells you, that the Lord ignites *a light*. He ignites the light of a candle, and that candle, wherewith the Lord ignites light in your body, is your soul.

Read it in Proverbs 20, 27: "The soul of man is the candle of the Lord, searching all the inward parts of the belly." Words somewhat strange, but which after this brief explanation will be sufficiently clear. For this proverb is also taken merely metaphorically for the heart (nature), but without reason.

Death is dark and somber.

When death has entered in, all light in us is gone out. God, Who is Lord of life and death, has then extinguished the light in our eye, and taken away the light that inwardly shone through our body.

It is all set in black, dark night.


ALSO with sickness and disease therefore our soul has a task to fulfill in our body.

Thus it renders service as a candle given us of God, inwardly to examine our body.

A characteristic, picturesque expression, by which to say, that by the sense (perception) of our soul we observe and feel what goes on inwardly in our body.

Feeling truly operates through our nerves, but feeling is located in those nerves themselves equally little, as a telegram hides in stretched electric wire.

If the nerves were not mysteriously related to the soul, and did the soul, by means of the nerves, not catch the emotions, you would not become aware of anything.

See it in the case of a man who has been chloroformed. Then the relation between his soul and his nerves has been lifted for a moment, and then a leg can be amputated, without his knowing anything about it.

Thus it is indeed your soul that renders service, to be on the watch for what goes on in your body, and now, as Bilderdyk so beautifully observes, it is *pain*, given us of God as a means to warn us, that conditions in the body are not what they should be.

By feeling, what we call, unwell, to have unpleasant sensations, or when it becomes worse, to become op-

pressed, to suffer pain, God the Lord causes you to discover by the candle of your soul, that it is not well
with you.

As a rule He even makes you discover by the candle
of your soul, *where* the wrong in your body hides, and
so enables you to tell the physician, what *he* himself
cannot see.

By that same candle of your soul He discovers it
to you, as soon as after strenuous labor the strength
of your body is exhausted; for then you become tired.
By that same candle of your soul He warns you, in case
by intemperate use of food or drink you might sin against
your body; for then you feel oppressed or dizzy. And
by that same candle of your soul He warns you, in like
manner, when you are seized by cold or sickness; for
then you feel indisposed.

VERY extensive therefore is the service, which, from the
side of the Lord, our soul renders also in and for our
body. For of course it also tells you, whether the means
you employ, for the restoration of your health, is effi-
cacious.

The glorious feeling when distress diminishes or
departs; when pain abates or at least grows less; when
feeling indisposed gives place to a more refreshing sense
of relief; and thus you observe that the medicine did
you good, it is all a knowledge of what goes on in your
body, which is brought you by your soul.

Hence *passive* insensibility about your body is not
willed by your God.

When in the dark inner chambers of your body He

ignites a candle, it is to *a purpose*. Then it is His will, that by that light you should see and observe what goes on in the mysterious hidden parts of your body. It is His will, that fortified by that knowledge, you shall so care for your body and so regulate your life, as is necessary, to insure your well-being. And also, when there appears to be trouble in the inner chambers of your body, that you will provide counsel, and shall apply the means of correcting what went amiss.

BUT that candle of the soul performs also more important services, first with respect to the life *that comes*, and presently with respect to the life that *goes under*.

First, with respect to the life *that comes*. For it is by the light that shines out from that candle in the inner chambers of the body, that a mother sees and loves her child, before it is yet born.

That wondrous, mysterious love, from which presently strength is born, to triumph over the sorrow, in which the child shall be brought forth; and from which some moments later the almost heavenly blessedness of mother-wealth is born, when she presses the little one to her heart, which only now she sees, and which yet she really already saw; which now for the first her eye beholds, and which yet is not strange to her. The little one, that she knew; with which she had lived already months together in blessed sympathy; and which long before he came, had won her love.

But then also when life *diminishes* and presently *departs*.

Commonly in the form, that one begins to feel old, and can no more do what once he did.

Then the Lord illumines us inwardly with that candle, and by that light we observe, that the house and in that house our inner chambers lose something of their original freshness, and this the Lord shows us, to tell us, that moderation becomes duty, that the body can no more be taxed to the extent of former days; more still, to warn us, that the body is running down, and that slowly the end approaches.

Sometimes also the Lord sends us those dread warnings while we are still in the strength of our life, when by that candle of our soul He makes us see, that in those hidden inner chambers there is a germ of corruption at work, which is incurable, and destined to break down our body, as is said, *before one's time*.

And wise is he, who does not treat this lightly, but lets himself be warned by his God, and prepares himself for the end, for the rapid unravelment which comes.

THERE are two things yet, which the candle of the Lord effects in our body. *Intimidating* is one, *comforting* the other.

When with that candle of the soul the Lord makes light in the darkness of our body, He is also the *Holy One*, and Who thereby discovers to our eye the bitter fruit of sin, which is observable in the inner chambers of the soul.

Sometimes the fruit of a passing sin, when, in whatsoever manner, we have gone beyond ourselves, and guilty weariness works its after effects. But sometimes also, the results of gross sins still work their aftermath, of sins of youth, or sins of mid-life.

He Who then holds the candle, is *our Judge*, Who wills that we should humble ourselves before His face.

But sometimes also that candle of the Lord in the inner chambers of our body brings blessed comforting.

Once indeed we must part from this body, and for a time our soul shall be *unclothed*.

But so it will not *continue*. Some day the Lord returns upon the clouds, and then every one that fell asleep in Jesus, receives his body back again in *glorious* form.

And of this also that candle of the Lord makes you conjecture something prophetic.

It shows you, that in your body also, mysterious and hidden, there is *something* that eternally abides.

## V

## "Neither Could Be Healed of Any"

### THE LORD OUR HEALER

THERE is in Scripture a hard word about our doctors, and that written by a doctor himself.

You remember Luke, the Evangelist, was a physician by profession. And yet of the woman, who touched the hem of Jesus' garment, he did not hesitate to write this brief *historia morbi*: She was a woman, who had had an issue of blood twelve years; who for the sake of recovery had spent all her living upon physicians; and who yet *could not be healed of any* (Luke 8, 43).

Mark, who was no doctor, lifts the veil yet a little higher, and in chapter 5, 26 adds, not only that she had spent all she had upon physicians, but that instead of having her bitter ailment grow better, it had become still worse. For so it literally reads, that she was a woman, "who had suffered many things of many physicians, and had spent all she had, and was nothing bettered, but *rather grew worse.*"

For our physicians hard, but nevertheless excellent words; which are well adapted to attune a doctor, who lives by God and His Word, to modesty and pity.

For what is here written, still occurs.

There are still sick people, who have spent a great deal upon physicians, without avail, and with whom, in spite of the pains they have suffered, things have not become *better*, but *worse*.

And also, though you take away the latter, which is always rare, it still remains an ever recurring fact, that he who suffers spends a good deal on physicians, and yet can be healed by none.

Time and again our physicians stand helpless over against much suffering and mortal danger.

The mysterious plague, prevalent in our times, shows it anew. They conjecture, they experiment, but in reality they face a mystery.

There is no disgrace in this, neither does it lessen our appreciation of their ability, when they *do* heal.

But there is an admonition in it for all physicians, not to think too highly of their art; and likewise an admonition for all sufferers, not to esteem their doctor as a god, who has their healing in his hand.

And this admonition is far from superfluous.

Time and again you see physicians, and professors of medicine, and medical councils appear with an authority and hear them speak in an apodictical tone, as though their insight were infallible and their medicine all-powerful.

They talk of an "official science" and call in the strong arm of the law, to impose it upon you.

They open their hospitals as some kind of temples, from whence a speech goes forth, as though there alone salvation were to be found.

And when they enter the house of the sick, you hear them not infrequently oracle in a tone, as though the life of the sufferer were not in God's power, but in *their* hand.

And while thus among our physicians so almost nothing is observed of the sense of their deep dependence upon God the Lord, even among the sufferers you find but a few, who in their sickness really trust in God, and see nothing in their physician save an "instrument in God's hand."

Especially they who have money, and thereby can obtain the help of foremost physicians and professors, or go to bathing places and softer climates, are for the most part so strongly under the impression that a doctor *can* and *must* heal everything, that in their physician they see a sort of god, and are angry with their doctor, when the ailment does not abate.

When not so long ago the report went abroad, that a certain Dr. Koch at Berlin had discovered a medicine for the cure of consumption, he was literally deified. Deified by consumptives who by trainfuls steamed to Berlin, and deified by the Government, which already made preparations to introduce a second sort of vaccination.

The sick do not think of God, but expect all their help from physicians, and these are they, who by their unbelief bring it to pass, that doctors come to behave themselves as demigods.

And even confessors of Christ, by no means so very rarely, take part in this infidel-like worship of the doctor.

Shall the medical profession on this account be condemned, and, as some have tried, practice healing without physicians, by laying on of hands, by anointing or by prayer?

Jesus says otherwise. His saying was: "They that are sick *have need* of the physician."

Moreover, the appearance of Christ brought us in this domain also *a gift of God.*

In the world without Christ the art of healing is still very backward. See it in China, at Java, in Africa, and elsewhere.

Only in that part of the world, that was baptized, medical science has come to higher development. And it may safely be said, that, had not Christ come, the art of healing would never have become, what it now is.

Very great therefore is the gift, which from Divine compassion has been given to the baptized nations, in the now so richly developed science of medicine, for the alleviation of much suffering.

To underestimate that gift, would not be honoring God, but a falling short in that thankfulness, which we owe God.

Only, as little as bread feeds you, if God does not bless it to you, just so little does medicine avail you, unless God the Lord directs the physician and blesses the medicine.

And where this simple, childlike truth is lost from sight by physician and by patient, "the gift of God" is used against God and to rid oneself of Him, instead of *to His glory.*

Do not complain therefore exclusively about impiety of our physicians, however much ground there may be for complaint about the materialism of very many physicians.

You can never take away the fact, that by their

unbelief the patients have made physicians as unbelieving as they are.

Our physicians go from one sick-bed to another, and if now as a rule they found their patients with their surroundings in that simple godly mood, which for the sick chamber is the best aroma, their daily presence amidst such surroundings would unobservedly inwork upon their own mood.

But this is so largely wanting.

In many circles all this is passed over with a smile. Even when one is mortally ill, dying must not be mentioned in his hearing.

We are convinced, that in case you yourself were a doctor, and you had made your twenty or thirty visits, it would impress you, how in most sick-rooms almost every expression of a more pious attitude of mind on the part of the sick and on the part of those who nurse them, is wanting.

There are even Christian homes where at other times Our Father in the heavens is counted with, but which, when the doctor comes, behave themselves, as though for the doctor's sake, every idea that the patient is not merely a sick body, but a sick *man*, must carefully be suppressed.

Surely, there are also other causes; but certainly the patients share a not insignificant part in the unbelief of our physicians.


IF now our physicians were able to heal *all* diseases, there would never come a turn in this.

When a man has the choice of taking refuge with the creature or with his God, by nature he chooses always the creature, *provided that creature but helps*.

See it in yourself with all those sicknesses, for which a sovereign remedy has been found.

Then almost no one thanks his God.

But since day by day there are still patients, by whose bedsides physicians stand powerless, so that they die; and since institutions are still crowded with incurables, and every time again epidemics go around, where medical aid falls short; in that very fact, however sad, *that so many cannot be cured, lies* the medicine against unbelief. A very bitter medicine, that early or late grows on the grave of every one of us.

Then there accompanies us to that grave insooth, the pastor, but *not* the physician. Simply because that pastor knows of a medicine also against death, while in the dying of his patient the physician reached the limit of his power.

But if matters are to improve in our sick-rooms, in our hospitals, upon our deathbeds and upon our graves, understand, O people of the Lord, that you first of all, and you most of all have to make an end of that barren lack of faith, wherewith times of sickness are lived through so frequently in your own circles.

Your faith must royally, must in Divine glory, on and at your sick-bed glisten again.

Not merely the faith, that asks for recovery from sickness and for deliverance from death, and which consequently, when recovery came, presently bleeds to death again.

No, but also, yea, above all else that pious, that tender, that heart-felt faith, that makes one go through every sickness in company with his God, and from pain and mortal anxiety also draws gains for eternity.

## VI

## *"A Lump of Figs"*

### HEALING BY MEANS

Is there always done for our sick what is possible, to ameliorate their suffering, to break the power of disease, and, as far as we are able, to watch in behalf of the preservation of their life?

Alas, there is no ground as yet for boasting all too highly, of the saving power, that goes out from our medical science. She certainly made brilliant discoveries, her operations arouse our wonder, and against more than one evil she has found a fixed method of treatment. But of the fourteen hundred million persons here on earth, at most one third are profited thereby. And even with that one third medical care is provided by municipal charities, and in the country by a factotum, that is still so bitterly insufficient, that really only in the case of those, who are able to pay more freely, can care be said to be somewhat adequate. And even then, what mistakes and neglects, which the sick all too frequently have to pay for with their life.

The saying therefore is common abroad: "That doctors help more people under ground than heal them." And though this may be somewhat exaggerated, yet it is sure, that the grace-gift of God, that is given us in medicine, does not spread by far the blessing, which it should spread.

For this reason it is altogether plain, that in sickness many people refuse to place confidence in means; that more than one makes slovenly use of means; and that here and there there are even those who systematically refuse to call in a doctor's aid.

This at least is far more clear and far more understandable, than that there are so many others and so many more, who forget their God, swear by their doctor, and rather put themselves into human hands, than that they should lean upon the Lord their God.

Asa, the otherwise so godly king, who in his old age sought his physicians more than his God, remains for all God's people in times of sickness and danger of death a solemn warning.

YET our sick should not be victims of the constant swaying of our soul on this point.

When Hezekiah lay deathly sick, what would it have been for the Lord our God, to heal this elect prince miraculously and without means?

And yet the Lord did not do so. Rather He sent His prophet to the sick king; and now Isaiah appears at his sick-bed, not to announce to him a miraculous something, neither to rouse him spiritually; but altogether prosaically, almost vulgarly, as it seems to us, in the name of the Lord to tell Hezekiah, that they must take . . . *a lump of figs* (Is. 38, 21).

Could it ever be revealed more clearly and more forcefully, that when the Lord our God intends to heal the sick, as a rule brings that healing about by a twofold, creaturely means. First, *in casu* by figs, which He Himself had made to grow, and in which He has created a strong extracting power; and secondly, by a human helper, by whose hand and care the figs were put upon the boil.

For what other purpose did God make also healing herbs to grow, and Himself prepare healing waters in so many springs, were it not, that with the help of all such means His sick children should fight against diseases and sicknesses?

Even lepers in Israel the Lord did not allow by any means to go about freely; but, that this dreadful disease should not come upon all the people, He Himself gave to and through Moses sternest ordinances to cut off every touch with leprous persons.

Sickness, even as death, is *from sin*. Diseases and pestilences are evil, destructive powers, that come upon us as consequence *of sin*. When once sin shall be done away, there shall also be no more sickness. So long as sin holds sway, sickness also continues to rage. And therefore it is one battle and one struggle, which on the part of God is laid upon us, against sin and misery, against spiritual and physical evil.

THEREFORE your sick also must be cared for with tenderness, but also with seriousness. And when they are seriously ill, so that they lie at the point of death, then from their moaning and sighing there goes out to you a call for deliverance, against which for no moment you must stop up your ears.

When you hear some one, in danger of drowning, scream for help, you will not think for a moment, of quietly walking along, in cold blood to go home, and there pray for that man, the while he is already long drowned. No; then an ejaculatory prayer is sent upward. On the part of the drowning one, a: "God help me!" and from your heart a: "God, help me save him!"; the while you reach out for a rope, a pole, a ladder, or you yourself jump into the water, as you realize your calling of God, to save that man from death; and presently, after you have been permitted to save him, to thank God for that blessing.

And why help that drowning person, who was a stranger to you, and leave your own wife, or your own child, who lie sick at home, to languish without help?

Is not dying dying, whether you see one dying in the water, or slowly die away on a bed of down?

For, of course, whether you save one by means of a rope thrown toward him or by quinine; by a pole, which he grasps, or with tincture of iron, which he swallows; all these together are *means,* which God places at your disposal, wherewith to fight for the life of your fellow-man.

An animal does not see this. Ten and more poles may be at hand, but no animal will hand one out to another animal, in danger of drowning. Not to animal, but to man God gave this insight. And therefore you are under the stress of the sixth commandment, responsible, for doing all in your power, to save the life of husband, wife, child or dependent.

To you it was entrusted, and if in this you are indifferent, it shall once be required at your hand.

AGAINST one sin only you should here be on your guard. You should not separate the *means* from your *God,* as though your hand had made it, and as though with this means you would fight against God, to save your sick *from the hand of the Lord.*

Therein and therein alone lies the evil abuse.

Then one thinks: God wants to kill my child, for God has made him ill; and with this medicine I will try to withdraw my child from God's killing power.

And that of course is wicked.

This must never be.

It is God Who kills, and God Who makes alive. Whoever has at any time been saved from the water, was saved therefrom by God. And whoever recuperated from sickness, was healed therefrom by God. And such remains the case, though God uses a man with a pole, to save a drowning person, and a physician with medicine, to heal the sick.

*In everything* is the Lord.

He is the Almighty in the plague, in the pestilence and in the sickness, but He is equally the Almighty in the physician, in the medicine, and in every one, that cares for your sick.

You may be used of Him as *second* cause, but He is and always remains the *first* cause, both in the evil, that threatens your life and in the medicine, whereby He will avert that evil.


IT is therefore no caring for the sick, as it ought to be in a Christian family, when the bed is made and medicine given with regularity, but without an equally conscientious calling upon the Most High and supplicating the God of all compassion.

Prayer without work is also in the sick-room a caricature of true piety; but work without prayer is especially at the sick-bed a deriding of the living God.

See it in the case of Hezekiah.

First you have in Isaiah 38, 10-20 his glorious prayer, and only after that the prosaic order of the lump of figs.

According to Deut. 8, man shall not live by bread alone; for if you have nothing but bread, and God does not bless that bread, you will yet perish from hunger.

And so the sick also shall not live by medicine alone, for all those medicines effect nothing, except, as God's almighty power operates in them.

To your medicine as to your bread applies what is written in Deut. 8, 17, 18: "Say not in your heart: My power and the might of my medicine has restored me to health; for thou shalt remember the Lord thy God, that it is He, Who gave you the medicine, to work its healing power in you."

With your medicine therefore pray, even as with your work. From your God, and from your God alone await recovery, if it pleases Him, by medicine to recover you from your sickness.

Prayer on your own part, and urging your sick to pray.

Your God, and Him alone to be magnified by your sick, and willingness yourself to be nothing but an instrument in His hand, but then also a willing instrument, that works accurately, as God wills that you shall work.

Your patient is perhaps sick unto death. And now

God wills to use you, to fight for his life. And therein will a child of God be tender of conscience, always zealous, and in a sacred sense self-sacrificing.

With a drowning person, who screams for help, but also with your sick, who moans upon his bed.

## VII

# "She Suffered Many Things of Many Physicians"

## OUR PHYSICIANS

THE physician has in the lives of many an all but too large a place, to which sometimes cleave sad remembrances, yea, which sometimes gave rise to bitter conflict of faith.

And this also Scripture intends, that you should consider, and therefore puts before us ever and again those tragic words from the narrative of the woman who had an issue of blood: "There was a woman, who had an issue of blood twelve years, and *had suffered many things of many physicians, and had spent all that she had, and was nothing* bettered, but rather grown worse" (Mark 5, 25).

Cutting words, and which to this day find their sad application. There are still those in all lands, who, going about with an hidden or incurable disease, have tried now one and again another physician, ever and again hoping that he would heal them, and who every time again were disappointed. They often suffered much, and underwent all sorts of artificial treatments and subjected themselves to all sorts of rules of life, and swallowed all sorts of medicine. And yet in the end their case was no different from that of this woman: much pay, no betterment, and not infrequently a further decline.

Herein you should not exaggerate. For over against

these sad cases there are a thousand others, in which the medical profession succeeded, in bringing about wonderful recoveries. Especially in our times medical science accomplishes great results. And healing of diseases, reports of which are frequently abroad, fill you with amazement.

The fact however remains none the less true, that also the medical science all too frequently proves to be a *broken reed*. And the bitter complaint and disappointment with respect to many physicians, is by no means always unfounded.

It is true, that the poor, not infrequently, are treated more hastily and carelessly, than the man of money. It cannot be denied that more than one woman died in childbed from an infection, communicated to her by the doctor. It is, alas, so, that many a doctor falls short in a proper investigation of the real character of the disease, and thereby applies a wrong medication. The list of complaints against doctors might be lengthened considerably.

But he who stands right in his faith, raises no objection against medical science, neither does he find fault with God, for allowing medical science to render us such imperfect service.

All relief and recovery, and this is incredibly much, which medical science brings us, is pure grace, that comes to us from the compassion of God.

By our sin we have appointed unto ourselves nothing save sickness and death.

And that which breaks that power of sickness and death for a time, or at least in part, is a free gift of your God, a balsam which He drops into the wound, which you yourself inflicted.

WE must be *governed* by men, and how loud the complaint about all sorts of mistakes on the part of the Government. By men the *Gospel* must be ministered unto us, and what suffering Christ's church has endured through all ages by reason of the heresies and highnesses and slovenlinesses of preachers. So must medical science be applied by men, by sinful men like our rulers and preachers, and is it then to be wondered at, that they also, who practice medicine among us fall short in all sorts of ways, and time and again disappoint you?

Has not God ordained, that of every one hundred men in any calling only very few are excellent, very many mediocre, and not a few beneath the same? Is not this true of all callings and positions? Why then should your doctors be an exception to this rule?

And as regards all sorts of *sinful* practices with your physicians, surely they are there. But with your mayors, lawyers, preachers, house-mothers and dependents are there no sundry sins of overestimation of self-importance, of careless dealings, of selfish motives and so much more?

And, if so, why then should your physicians make an exception to this general human rule?

We grant you, they are no better, but they are certainly no worse than other people. There can only a few among them be brilliant, and to all sorts of sins they are subject even as you.

And the fact remains which cannot be denied: God has given you medical science as a gift of His compassion, but He lets it be ministered unto you by imperfect and always sinful men.

THUS the snag for the faith consists in this alone, that again and again we separate the Lord our God and His gift, and sometimes place them one over against the other.

With diseases of known and less serious character, it is trust in the doctor alone, and there is no calling upon God. When it assumes more serious aspects, and the art of the physician falls short, refuge is sought in prayer and others are asked to intercede.

And this antithesis God's child must not maintain.

That was the sin of King Asa, of whom it is written so sharply: Yet in his disease he sought not to the Lord, but to the physicians (II Chron. 16, 12).

And this must not be. This is godless. So doing you slight your Father Who is in heaven.

No, His is every medicament, which He created, and which He allowed man to discover, and His likewise the art and the science, the discretion and the insight, wherewith He has enriched the physician.

Medical science is no human, and far less an evil, demoniacal art, but a means given of God in His compassion to man to fight against sickness and death.

It is therefore a spiritual mistake to think: "I will call no physician and swallow no medicine, but I will pray, and without means God can heal me." For to keep you in life, God the Lord has no need of food. So you might just as well say: "I will buy no food, and refrain from nourishment. God can keep me in life." And so He can, but He does not do so, because He Himself has ordained it otherwise, and has said: "In the sweat of thy face thou shalt eat bread."

And even as God makes bread grow, so He created that multitude of herbs and drugs, which stop all sorts of disease in your body, and it is He, Who in that domain also endows His Aholiabs with knowledge.

Only, woe to you, if you use medical science apart from God, and do not pray that He bless it to your good, and do not give thanks, when He has so blessed it.

And woe likewise to the physician, who instead of ministering this gift of God as a priest of mercy, counts without God, and proudly boasts, that his power and the cunningness of his hand has wrought it.

THEREFORE let the people, that fear God, be not too impatient with the sometimes brutal unbelief of many doctors. God's children themselves in this matter have all too often set doctors the pace in unbelief.

Forget not, to our physicians, the temptation to fall away from God, is very great. Their study is almost altogether material. The school, in which they are trained, has no knowledge of God. And, also, a very great power is put into their hand.

And what has the church of Christ, what have believing people done, to cause our doctors to be humble before God?

Is it not almost nothing? Worse yet, by smallness of faith and by unbelief on the part of many a child of God on his sick-bed, many a doctor has lost all reverence for the faith.

This can and shall become different.

Also upon medical science before long the breath of the Christian life shall go forth. Christ and the physician shall not always remain separated.

But even if it comes to this, do not think that

therefore sin shall be brought to nought in our doctors, nor that therefore their imperfection shall be ended.

Even then many a physician will make mistakes. Even then carelessness and neglect will occur. Even then many a patient will not be healed of the doctor. And even then many a sick person will die, who, spoken humanly, with better treatment might have been spared.

But though this compels you, in the choice of your physician not to go to work too light-heartedly, yet let this not shake your faith, neither let it embitter you.

For you know, that the gift of God, which you call medical science, cannot be ministered unto you by angels, and that, since it must be ministered to you by men, you find your own human imperfection and sin back again also in your physicians.

But above all, by calling in a doctor, you do not fall beyond the reach of God's providence.

Whatever the doctor may do, it is His hidden will, that becomes evident, and His counsel that shall stand.

No physician, whoever he be, can take an ell from the length of any one's life or add to it.

And therefore do not embitter your heart by such troublous thoughts and poison not your soul.

The Lord reigns, and it is He alone, Who cuts off the thread of our life and the thread of the life of our loved ones.

## VIII

## *"Like a Weaver His Web"*

### SUDDEN DEATH

UNEXPECTEDLY to be overtaken by serious illness, and suddenly to face death, is an evil, against which the prayer of even the most devoted of God's children goes out.

More pious kings than Hezekiah have not sat on David's throne, and yet, when Hezekiah became at once deathly sick and he suddenly came to face the valley of the shadow of death, he complained and groaned before his God, and the Lord was moved by the prayer, to remove the plague from him and to save him from death.

So he spoke later in his prayer of thanksgiving: "Like a crane or a swallow, so did I chatter; I did mourn as a dove: mine eyes lifted themselves on high to the Lord" (Is. 38, 14. Dutch version).

It was dreadful to him to see his life loosen itself from him, and it seemed to him as though God cut him off, as a weaver his web.

Whatever the nature of the plague was that troubled him, Hezekiah knew that it was the Lord, Who took hold of him in his sickness, threw him down, and now from moment to moment was busy, in taking away his life from him, and to destroy his earthly existence. Therefore he exclaimed even twice: "From day even to night wilt thou make an end of me" (Is. 38, 12), as though he felt, that, if the plague were not removed, he would no more fetch the evening.

Hezekiah fell thus in God's hand.

He himself saw the malignant boil, that threatened to poison his blood; and he truly made use of the means, advised him by Isaiah, by putting a lump of figs upon the festering swelling; but with all this Hezekiah clearly sensed, that he had to do with his God; that God was in the plague; and that the arm of the Lord weighed heavily upon him, to oppress him even unto death.

THIS stands written also for your sake.

Not that you might hope for a miracle, as took place with Hezekiah. There is no more prophet on earth, who, like Isaiah, brings you revelations from God, regarding your lot in life and the hour of your death.

A promise of still fifteen years of life, as came to Hezekiah, cannot occur now. And a sign such as was given Hezekiah, that the shadow on the sun-dial went back ten degrees, has, after Revelation was once ended and thus closed, never fallen to the share of any one.

Do not therefore in such dreadful moments detain your soul with this. That would be the abuse of God's Word; confusing yourself with fanaticism; and would end in nothing, save bitter, crying disappointment, till at length you would anyway, but then in despair, go into death.

But from Hezekiah learn, that with all such plagues you at once perceive clearly, that you have to do with the Lord your God; and turn yourself with all your agony of death, cast yourself with all the anxiety of your soul, without hesitating for one moment, upon your Covenant-God.

Not first all sorts of other things, and then, when all that other does not help, at length appeal to God. No, but at the first approaches of anxiety, at the first trembling at death, at once seek your refuge with the Holy One, and in your deathly sickness itself you will feel the dreadful hand of God's holy majesty.

In moments of such deep gripping seriousness watch especially against all division and doubleness in your soul. Hezekiah felt God's almighty hand in the throbbing of the malignant boil. He felt how God was already busily engaged, in cutting, as a weaver his web, the texture between his body and his soul. He felt presently, how God's power operated in that lump of figs, to draw this poison from the boil. And just because he was aware of God all around him, saw God's power in that plague and in that medicine, therefore he did not let go of God for one moment, but called and moaned, and refreshed his troubled soul in fellowship with his Shepherd and his God.

In all such moments of agony of death that suddenly come upon you, it all depends therefore upon *piety of heart*. And that piety of heart you cannot at that moment suddenly as by magic work in your soul, but in that critical hour you can let it operate in you only, *when a truly pious life lies back of you*. Piety taken in its deepest sense, that in your soul consciously you continually practice fellowship with the Eternal Being.

To miss that fellowship, and ability to endure that lack of fellowship with the Eternal Being, is in God's children deepest sin.

Then one lives hours together, half a day, sometimes a whole day, without so much as a thought of the Name of the Lord passing through the soul. In everything busy, one forgets his God, and lives without Him. And then, yea, then prayer is made, and hymns of praise are sung; but even in prayer thoughts wander, and in song words are uttered, in which the soul has no part.

And, of course, when amidst such conditions Death suddenly climbs in at your window, and with the death sweat already on your forehead you lie down upon your bed, the soul becomes confused, and cannot at once inlive in a piety, which is foreign to it.

The body then demands so dreadfully much of the soul. Thousand questions storm through the troubled heart. Everything about you frightens you. And you tremble with fear at the knowledge so suddenly thrust upon you, that you are to die.

And then everything divides itself before you. On one side the deadly plague, and the physician, and the medicine, and all that people do, to come to your help; and far away from all this, high above you, that God Whom you had forgotten, and to Whom you now call, but with a muffled sound, that despondingly falls back upon your own soul.

And this was spared Hezekiah. He too wept and cried like a child, he too chattered as a swallow, and all his crying was, that God might spare him; but his God was no stranger to him. To the eye of his soul it was all one: the power of God in his plague; the hand of his God busy to cut off his life; the working of his

God in that lump of figs; and the listening ear of his God, in fatherly compassion, ready to hear the complaint of his soul.

MOST trying is such a sudden facing of death, when it overtakes you when *you are alone*, as often happens in case of a shock, or accident. The most dreadful above all, when, as often happens in great cities with its high buildings, fire breaks out and the way out is obstructed, and one faces the flame, which encroaches upon him, and there is no way of escape.

This is already far less, when a pestilence breaks out. Not as though this were not dreadful; but because such an epidemic plague *sends its messenger ahead.*

Days, weeks before you hear from far-off lands, that the plague is approaching, and that God the Lord sent out the angel of His wrath, to call the nations to seriousness and to rouse them from their sleep of death.

And herein is a grace of your God, which you must not despise.

For then He does not overtake you as a lion, which leaps upon his prey, but warns you from afar, tells you that He is coming; and cries: *"To-day, while you hear my voice."*

Herein is this compassion, that thereby your God offers you the opportunity, to prepare yourself for the worst. That in case you had unaccustomed yourself to your God, you turn again to Him. That in case you had estranged yourself from your God, to turn away from your wanderings, and seek again His holy fellowship.

A grace, that avails nothing with respect to the

world which hardens itself, but which so often gave the glorious impulse to unstable souls, which ever yet hesitated, to bring about heart-felt and definite conversion. And a grace, which, above all, always showed itself so effective in calling God's children, who had sunken away into apathy, back to a condition of living, sensitive piety.

AND O, then that return to humble, sensitive piety on the part of God's saints bears again such beautiful fruit.

Not alone in that they heed again the commandments of God, and thus also according to the sixth commandment, they avoid and prevent everything, whereby recklessly they might endanger their own life or the life of their neighbor; but above all, that in everything, they begin to see their God again in the plague that approaches; in the prosperity, which they still enjoy; in the life of wife and children; more still in the inner motions of their soul.

Then thought is taken again of God; then there rises again, also when the lips are silent, a song of praise for His infinite compassion in the Son of His love; and then the soul is moved to pray without ceasing, that God's hiddenness might again be upon our tent, and our own soul and the soul of our dear ones might be prepared, in case He so appoints it, to meet our God also in His bitter wrath.

And if then it pleases God, to overtake us with His plague, or take away from our home, as a sheep is snatched from the fold, then the transition in our soul is no longer needed. Then death as it comes is no more a thief that breaks in and surprises us, but a messenger from our God, whose arrival we have expected. Then there is fellowship with the Eternal Being, even when things are at their blackest, even when the waves and billows of the Almighty go over us. Yea, then our soul knows, that even death cannot separate us from that fellowship, but on the contrary brings it to us yet more intimately, and then forever.

## IX

## *"Going as He Came"*

IN days of seriousness nothing tunes the heart to a mood so somber, as the pressing thought, that our life, our being, our whole existence upon earth has failed of its purpose.

The cutting word of Jesus to Martha: "Thou art troubled about many things, one thing is needful," then disturbs our conscience, and you cannot smother the painful question: What have I lived for? What fruit did my existence bear? What is the particular gain of my existence as man?

More than one interprets this reproach of conscience in an altogether wrong way.

One is told of what a Moses wrought, of what a St. Paul accomplished, and of what even now many a man of power and talent effects before the eye and ear of all, and then so readily commits the fault, of comparing one's own work to the work of such men. And of course, since, with a few notable exceptions, the greater majority is not called to public labors of this sort, but was given the task to render humble service in an household, in a trade or office, in a school or store, one is readily inclined to complain by reason of this, that his life was spent to no purpose.

And, as you see at once, this is altogether wrong. When God Himself has so disposed our human life and has so instituted it, that ninety-nine out of every hundred are called to no other than this ordinary daily labor; and also that for the doing of this extensive labor it requires ninety-nine out of every hundred, then every one, who, called to this labor has performed the same, has not lived to no purpose, but on the contrary has responded to his life's end.

So beautifully and correctly therefore did our fathers name every one's circle of activity, *his divine calling,* and it neither befits nor behooves you, ever to look down slightingly or arrogantly upon this your divine calling. On the contrary, you must exert yourself with respect to it; apply yourself to it; with your whole person be devoted to it. What you do, must be done well. And every one is obliged and beholden, in his divine calling to put the talent given him of God to usury.

Thus, that you might know, whether the sad complaint of the Preacher (Eccl. 5, 15): "Going as he came, and thus lived for nought," is applicable to you, you should ask yourself the threefold question: Not only *what you did;* but also *what you became;* and no less what has become of *what God entrusted to you.*

Only in these three together does life's purpose reach its goal.

We begin with the last, because by his saying: "Going as he came," the Preacher refers to our goods, our property, our estates. He introduces it by saying: "As he came forth of his mother's womb, naked shall he return," and follows it up with the words: "He shall take nothing of his labor, which he may carry away in his hand."

Also in that property lies for a part the purpose of

our life. All our goods together form the wealth of the whole world, and God gave this to the children of men, that they should direct and put it to usury to His glory. And, reckoned by a life-time, that wealth is by no means so very small. A common workman, who from his twentieth to his sixtieth year earns ten dollars a week, saw himself by reason of this alone entrusted with already twenty thousand dollars.

And it is as the Preacher says: one can possess this good all these years in such a way, that at his death nothing of it goes with him.

But he who has been a disciple of his Savior, is differently conditioned. From his youth up he has understood the call: "Lay up for yourself a treasure in heaven, where neither moth nor rust doth corrupt," and learned the sacred art of giving in such a way, and of so giving alms, and of so putting his money to usury in behalf of the service of the Lord, that at his death a whole capital was laid up, not on earth but above.

Whether he who laid up that capital was a rich man, who gave away more than one hundred thousand dollars, or a poor widow, who offered her two mites, makes no difference. Jesus Himself said, that this poor widow had cast in more than all the others. For, that heavenly capital does not reckon after the cipher of money, but after the white-heat of the power of faith, that operated in your life.

But at all events, he who so spent his goods, does *not* go as he came, and most certainly takes a fruit of this his labor of soul with him.

He has not spent his all; he has something left over, and all that rich possession, which he laid over is safely deposited and laid up by his Father Who is in heaven.

He who neglected this in his life-time, usually tried to make it up before or at his death, by making bequests of what he had. And surely, that is the duty of the delinquent, and better than nothing. But yet, the true power of faith, from which the treasure above is laid up, is the liberal expenditure of your gold or of your mites in the midst of life, when, that you might give, you deny yourself something.

This then is the first question you have to answer; but yet more serious is the second, the forceful gripping question: *What you became?*

Alas, there are many, who when it comes to dying, do not enter upon eternity richer, but poorer; who did not increase and advance, but decreased and spiritually shrank.

This is evident, when one is so sadly affected by remembrances of his youth, when the heart was far less evil and the tendency toward good so much stronger; when in later years one did so much and various kinds of things, from which one would have shrank in earlier years; and when a troubled feeling haunts us of having grown weaker in will-power, stronger in selfishness, less noble in one's own deliberations.

Then upon the troublous question: *What you became?* must follow the bitter answer: *Ever less.* And your dying speaks of a pitiful loss of human capital, not as regards the world, which is then delivered from you, but with respect to your own being, to your own character, to your soul and your person.

Then you go not as you came, but *less* than when you were born. Then your life brought you no gains, but you have lived to your own *hurt*.

But even if your conscience does not reproach you of such a loss, and though you remained about what you always were, even then your life did not fulfill its purpose. You have all your life long buried the capital of your person, the treasure of your existence in the dust of everydayness, and now at your death you are raked up again as a dead coal from those ashes.

This would have been so, if immediately at your birth you had died, and thus had not lived upon earth, so that even so your life is lost, has been frittered away and spent for nought.

Nothing has been gained; nothing in self-control, nothing in character, nothing in love, nothing in will-power, nothing in compliancy and fitness for life.

You have perhaps become more capable, more crafty, more worldly-wise and practically more usable; but all this belongs to the things, which we leave here, which do not go along with us, which do not follow us into eternity. All this passes away.

And, therefore, you can look back upon your life with thankfulness and gladness, only when, as compared to the past, you observe that with the five talents other five talents have been gained; that you have increased; and that now fuller and mightier in you is the power to resist sin; to repress your selfishness in love; to deny yourself and not your God.

They who have so lived, and have so worked, of them the Spirit saith: *"And their works do follow them."*

YET sometimes in this respect also, during the brief weeks, that precede dying, wondrously much is made up.

He who never believed, sometimes in the face of approaching death has believed. He who most sought himself, with the outlook upon his end, has begun to think of others. He who thus far was irritable and gave way to passion, has been seen sometimes even on his deathbed or in the sick-room to come to self-control.

Not that here everything is gold that glitters.

Nowhere more than in the sick-room is counterfeit manufactured, and every one knows of instances, where persons in fear of death, became, O, so gentle and so kind, and who in spite of this, when God healed and restored them, soon showed themselves the same old sinners as before.

But as readily as we grant this, and as seriously as by reason of this we warn against self-deception, yet equally readily the fact must be acknowledged, that there are also sick-rooms and deathbeds, that can speak of miracles of grace. There are those who have gone from the sick-room rich and blessed, who were, O, so godless and unbelieving when they were first taken. And there are also those who have returned to the world recovered from sickness, who were healed not merely after the body, but also renewed in the soul.

Those weeks or days that you lie down helplessly, *need* not therefore be lost. On the contrary, they can bear rich fruit. Fruit that remains.

AND so of itself you have the key in hand for the third question: *What you did.*

For see, our deeds on earth are so relative. The world's course is directed by God the Lord, and things about us are established far more of themselves than by us. Our part therein is so small and insignificant. Even of a Nebuchadnezzar Scripture says, that he was nothing but a saw, which God drew.

But there is another *action*, that in far higher sense goes out from you, and that is the moral power you have shown; the influence for good, that went out from you; the seeds of godliness and piety, which you have sown in the hearts of others; the animation of your word; the comfortings of your love; the help you offered others in the conflict of their soul.

These are works that remain, and which follow you as you go down into the grave, and these are the works, which every one can do, man or woman, young or old, whether one is rich, or whether one is poor.

In that nobler work you can also have your part in the sick-room, when you lie down, and continue therein until your latest breath, by pouring out from your heart into the soul of others, what is poured out in you by the Holy Ghost.

## X

## *"Drawn Near Unto the Gates of Death"*

### THE PLAGUE OF GOD *

EPIDEMICS, at times, occasion very great mortality (Ps. 107, 18). In some regions more than double the ordinary. Even such that grave-diggers have had to ask help and undertakers were not equal to their somber task.

And far greater yet, comparatively, is then the number of *the sick*. In one village, as reported, there were two thousand confined to their beds, while there were but a little over one thousand left, who were not stricken.

This might make a deep impression, you would say. Fear will come upon an entire population. The joy-fires of sensual pleasure will be extinguished. A call will go out on every hand for a day of fasting and prayer!

And yet, the state of the public mind does not respond to this expectation. Newspapers indeed are full of the plague when it goes around. It is the subject of common conversation. It is not laughed at nor ridiculed as has been done before. But as by a higher power the population is by no means impressed.

At least he who has witnessed in the place of his habitation a serious cholera—or smallpox—epidemic, and still vividly remembers what terror and fear had taken hold of every heart, will readily have to confess, that while now an occasional note of deeper seriousness is struck, heartfelt emotion on the part of the masses is not in evidence.

* Written at the time of Influenza Epidemic.—*Tr.*

And do you ask, how to explain this just think of the incredibly great number of *cases*, in proportion to which the number of *deaths* seems so small.

When cholera was about, sometimes more than half the number of cases was fatal; with La Grippe at most one in fifty.

Thus danger is *less* pronounced. By far the most that are taken, recover.

Another cause of the lesser emotion is, that this plague does not have that frightfulness, that violence, that hideousness in its method of attack. As long as it does not infect the lungs, it is mostly even very light.

Psychologically therefore it is altogether explainable, that with the masses there is no deep stirring of emotion.

Something about which he alone makes complaint, who with great epidemics over-estimated the merit of such emotion.

For then, when suddenly every voice of gladness was silenced, and sensual pleasure was done for, and churches could not hold the multitudes, the man of superficial judgment, took this for conversion, and deemed himself able to prophesy better times for the Kingdom of God.

But scarcely did the plague abate, but this prophecy proved false; and no sooner was the danger past, but it seemed, that the astonished multitudes were bent upon making good past losses, so wildly did wantonness break out again.

And yet, what was this reaction from the *un*natural austerity other than *natural?*

No; "sorrow toward God" is yet something altogether different from fear of the smiting hand of God.

Terror of possible death before the day is over works no true conversion.

All that threatens from without, remains outside of the kernel of the life of our soul. And as in the midst of shipwreck the sailor calls upon God, and presently, when saved, drinks himself drunk again with a curse upon his lips, so is also the multitude that knows not God, and yet momentarily has trembled before His Majesty.

BUT it is different with persons, young and old, who indeed have long been *regenerated*, and have never been able to convert themselves to the living God, once and for all, with all their heart and with all their soul.

Upon such in times past God has inworked very strongly by such a plague, and the number is by no means small of these spiritually born, but yet ever spiritually sleeping ones, who in such days of seriousness felt at once the fire burning in their bones, and could no longer resist, when the call went forth: "Awake, thou that sleepest, and let Christ be your light" (Eph. 5, 14).

It was then not the sickness that did this, for neither cholera, nor typhoid, nor influenza can ever bring one to conversion. Conversion always takes place through the Word, that as an hammer finally breaks the stony heart into pieces.

But what such a plague can do, is to make the blow of that hammer stronger, and bring to pass, that the Word takes hold of us more forcibly, that it enters more deeply into us, and leaves behind a more real impression with us.

And so also in any raging plague the call goes out to all in our midst who are regenerated, but not as yet converted, that finally for once they will open the eye of their soul to the highness of their Covenant-God; that they will make an end to that will-less halting between two thoughts; that now they will make choice between the service of the world and the service of Jesus; and that, to-day while you hear His voice, you will arise and go to your Father, and say: "Father, I have sinned against heaven and against Thee!"

In this coming to conversion at length of those who have so long postponed their conversion, the plague of God's hand must bear fruit to the honor of His Name.

And woe, woe Church of God, if that ripe fruit is not forthcoming.

BUT there is more.

To them also, who have their first conversion already behind them, there comes in an epidemic a serious admonition.

For it is untrue, that a first conversion is always followed by a steady increase in humble piety. One may so reason it and so represent it, but it is not so. Rather such continuous fruit of the first conversion is extremely rare.

It is almost the common rule, that, as soon as the first conversion has become somewhat a matter of the past, a wretched coolness ensues; and that, in the confidence that the matter of one's salvation is now settled, one dozes off again and begins to accustom himself to a half-hearted life, half pious but also half sinful. As though things could go on between God and our soul upon an unholy understanding.

And upon such sinful conditions among God's people, such a voice of God as goes forth in an epidemic, can exert so wholesome an influence.

Then God's child comes to repentence. He will have nothing more to do with his unholy dream, his sinful self-deception.

No, no, that is not serving the Lord his God with *all* his heart and *all* his soul.

That antagonizes what he chose in his conversion.

That is playing with the holy, which bears no further toleration.

And then you see the repentent sinner rise and shake off his bonds, and break with his lukewarmness and his hidden sin, and there is joy among the angels of God over so glorious an awakening of soul.

And then this precious gain breeds of itself yet another fruit.

Something begins to stir through the forest. A breath of life is wafted upon God's garden. Among all the company of God's faithful ones it comes to a renewing, a refreshing, an heightening of spiritual life.

It is as though preaching becomes more animated and plays in a key of higher seriousness. The service of prayer becomes more heartfelt. The gifts of compassion flow more freely.

There is more loosening of bands and a stronger drawing of cords that bind us to heaven.

The people have more love, and that warmer love of the Eternal fosters of itself warmer mutual love.

In the families levity is tempered. Quiet piety again spreads its gleams. It is as though the thunderstorm, that broke loose, has purified all of our spiritual atmosphere.

AND finally the thought, *that you must prepare your soul,* is more clear to you.

For though it is true that fear of death works no conversion, and that a piety, born merely from terror of the grave, misses the stamp of godliness; this does not take away, that he who is converted and fears his God, when he comes so near to the gate of death, is of himself pressed and compelled to *a preparation of his soul.*

It is indeed better that you are *always* prepared, and though your Lord comes as a thief in the night, you are not overtaken. But with most people this is not so.

For most people from life to death is always yet a dreadful transition.

And though you were then spared, so that from the very gate of death you were permitted to go back into life, the fruit of that preparing of your soul can be so precious.

Then you have once more meditated upon your life. You have asked yourself again, whether you have put the talent entrusted to you to usury. You have thought again of your obligation to your church, your country and your family.

And if then once again a new way of life opens before you, you walk differently; with firmer tread; more to the honor of your God!

## XI

## *"The Time of My Dissolution Is at Hand"*

### CONCEAL NOTHING

MAY I, must I acquaint some one, of whom I know, that his sickness is fatal, with his real condition?

Let this question be put not merely with respect to our consumptives, but in general, to all patients who are sick with incurable, quickly terminating diseases. And then you know, what most of our physicians, and with our physicians most families think about it.

*Concealment* is their watchword.

Let no one judge this practice too harshly. Both with our physicians and with our families, from their standpoint, there operates a higher motive.

Our physicians know by experience, that so little can be done with their patients, the moment they lose courage. Hope brings life, and so long as the glorious outlook upon recovery stimulates courage, the patient does not mind his suffering so greatly and struggles through his restless nights and lengthy days with more moral will-power.

And as regards the families, they mostly deem that *love* forbids, to tell the sick and slowly dying at once the full, hard truth.

Their beloved sick would be so frightened by it; perhaps burst out in bitter tears; and all the after days be prey to black despair.

Now it takes much effort on their part, to practice

self-control, and with sorrow in the heart, yet always to appear at the bedside with a hopeful smile. But love demands that sacrifice, which they are willing to bring.

And now it gives them pleasure, when they observe, how, thanks to their tactful silence, the poor patient continuously builds castles for himself in the air.

First, in winter time be on the lookout whether the swallows are not yet bringing summer back, and presently in sharp days of autumn look forward again to the cheerful fire on the hearth.

Always hope, always ideal illusions! Till finally death surprises them. But then, thanks to concealing love, the terror and the fear of dying has been spared them.

THERE's something more to this.

Especially of consumptives it has been observed, how little they themselves believe in their approaching death. At least so long as it has not gone too far, a consumptive is naturally cheerful. And though you tell him that his end is at hand, it is not often he believes it.

At least a consumptive who is in the twenties, as a rule, observes what ails him. He has frequently heard the signs of consumption discussed or observed with others. Nothing therefore would be more simple than that, observing these same phenomena with himself, he would at once draw the conclusion and understand whither things were going with him.

And when a consumptive does this, he well knows, that his condition is most serious. What Dr. Koch thought was a cure for consumption, did not prove, alas, to be the real, the of God appointed antidote. And unless one can take a timely departure for the North, and continue to live in the North, such a sick person well knows, that having reached a certain stage, consumption as a rule terminates quickly.

And yet, however strange it may seem, most consumptives do not apply this to themselves; and though it be, that they begin to fear the worst, yet hope keeps them ever confident, that with them, perchance, recovery will follow.

And with this in mind, even a pious physician, and they who desire to conceal the character of the disease ask, whether in the very nature of the disease God does not give an indication, *not* to tell our weakening patients that death is at hand.

Now in Christian families the opposite line of behavior is followed. When in our human way we foresee with some certainty, that our sick will die, we tell them so.

We do this with the aged, and also with young men and young women, whom God the Lord calls away early. Yea, even with our little children, if it pleases Him, to take them from us.

God's children even counted it a fault on the part of their physician, when they thought, that he tried to mislead them; and among God's people he will be sought after mostly as a physician, who himself is averse to false appearances, and plainly and simply "speaks the truth to his neighbor," and thus also to his patients.

And what else accounts for this difference, except this: that a child of God does not like to be deceived himself, and to be held ignorant of the fact, if he himself were nigh to death.

As well in our own circles as in those of the others we act therefore after the rule of the high commandment: "Therefore all things whatsoever ye would that men should do unto you, do ye even so to them" (Matt. 7, 12).

Only, for oneself one has another desire.

In those other circles one would wish for himself, not to hear about it, before it came to dying. And therefore they say nothing about it to their patients. In the circles of God's people, on the other hand, one would think it terrible, not to be told at once; and for this reason one would neither dare nor desire to conceal it from his patients.

CAN you now say, therefore, that those tragic patients, whose dying in the near future seems to be certain, in our circles are so much worse off?

Put the facts before you as they are.

When everything must be held back, for weeks and months together, there is played a kind of tragedy around their sick-bed. Nothing more is natural. Neither the fold in the face, that sets itself into a forced laugh; nor the tone of voice, which keeps conventionally cheerful; nor the content of the words, which contain a lie. A false attitude is dominant, in which every member of the household must take part, and in which they who come in from without, are introduced. It is agreed beforehand, what shall be said, how the condition shall be presented, while the physician takes the leading rôle in the tragedy, himself taking part.

But even when the patient does not see through that game altogether, you understand, that a patient who is but somewhat more discerning, becomes aware of something strange; from that continuous play receives a queer impression; and therefore is by no means yet contented.

Hence the numerous inquiries, and the stare with searching eyes upon the physician and those that stand by; as though he would say: *"But, Doctor, you are not deceiving me?"*

And when a visitor comes in, he is mostly accompanied by a member of the household, to prevent a possible betrayal of the game; but when for but one moment that poor patient is alone with such a visitor, one hears at once the question put: *"I am not going to die, am I?"*

But listen, the door opens; one of the family is just come upstairs again; and to the question faintly caught there sounds the answer, not from the visitor, but from mother or sister: "No, indeed, my darling; what are you thinking of! The doctor was ever so satisfied."

And he who writes this, has sometimes heard this lie iterated and reiterated, when ten hours after, he who asked it, was already in eternity.

Is it not dreadful, when for weeks or months together, in the gravest that can overtake us, from love, be it so, and with the best of intentions a play is acted out with us, where the need was so very great, to prepare our soul, and might it be, to spread a blessing around us?

Can this be good in the sight of God, to involve all our family, and every one that comes in, in such a systematic untruth? Can it be good for our heart, to show ourselves so many days smiling, when in our heart we weep? And above all, is it permissible, that we allow our poor patients in such a way to be surprised by death, and without transition, without comforting light, let them pass into eternity?

Moreover, is this honoring God's creature in your patient, when you deem that he could not bear the knowledge of death, and would not be able to endure it, if he knew that his dissolution was at hand?

*May* a father so deal with his baptized child, a mother with her darling, whom she received from God? Death is anyhow sure to come. On the part of your sick, if they must die, there is nothing more to hope for from this world. And of eternity, wherein their only expectation can lie, you tell them nothing, and you prepare them no blessed entrance.

And, therefore, though we do not judge harshly, and though we misinterpret no one's intentions, yet with a lie at the sick-bed you come upon something cowardly, something untrue, something unmanly, that makes you say: "This cannot be good before God."

He who is about to die, *must* in the first place know it himself (2 Tim. 4, 6).

AND now come into our circles, and see how things there are done.

No, boasting is not seemly, and sometimes in our circles also consumptives die away slowly, whose sick-bed was far from inspiring, and with whom no spark of courage, born of the holy faith, glistened.

Alas, also in our circles faith is not the portion of all. There are also such as are hardened of heart.

But this can be testified to the praise of God's grace, that as a rule this is different. And that our poor patients, whom we do not mislead, and who therefore know that they are to die, after the first shock, which such knowledge always brings with it, they rather are glad that they know it.

And, O, then there is such a change in the feeling of the heart. Now that nothing more is to be expected of earth, the eye directs itself so much more fixedly to heaven. Of the world one becomes weaned, and with God and His dear Son and His holy angels the more intimate. Not infrequently it happens, that our patients soon end the bitter struggle, and now calmly and resignedly await what God appoints them. And meanwhile, confident in their Savior, drink in draught after draught from the cup of His blessed comfortings.

Also, from such a sick-bed, there goes out a refreshing influence upon the whole family. With a sort of sacred emotion one approaches the sick-bed and feels himself more seriously affected. So there comes higher, holier peace upon the heart of all.

And when at length there comes the moment of parting, both he who dies and he who stands by the bedside, are prepared for it, and oftentimes God privileged those who remained behind to jubilate: "A crown is laid up for him."

## XII

## *"Carry Him to His Mother"*

### THE SICK CHILD

A SICK *child* is so altogether different from a sick adult.

In Holy Scripture also this is evident with the sick children, of which we are told, with the sick little boy of David and the sick little daughter of Jairus; and even more still, with the little boy of the Shunammite in the days of Elisha.

That little boy may have been six or seven years old, for he had gone out from home alone to the land, where his father was at work; and yet he cannot have been much older, for his mother held him for hours on her knees.

This little boy had gone in the morning to the field where father and the men were reaping. The walk had evidently been too much for him. It had brought on a great, serious congestion. His little head began to pain him sorely; and when he came to his father, his first cry was: "O, father, my head, my head!" (II Kings 4, 20).

Yet the father saw nothing serious in it. At least he went on with his work, and had the boy carried home by a servant, *to his mother*.

A sick child, he rightly felt, belongs with mother. But already on the way the trouble increased. The unsteady motion occasioned by being carried, added to the increasing heat, seems to have aggravated the congestion. And when he finally came to his mother, the Shunam-

73

mite took him on her lap and put his head, that pained him so, against her breast. And so he remained, without help or counsel, until noon; and later in the afternoon the boy probably had a convulsion, and in that convulsion he died.

And only then she took the yet warm little corpse from her lap, and laid her little child on the bed in the prophet's chamber of Elisha.

In such a child already that quiet, willing, almost silent suffering affects one so tragically.

That crying: "My head, my head!" is all the sound he made, and quietly he lets himself be carried away; feels the pain less, so he might but rest on mother's lap, and without another groan, he dies.

When sickness comes, we older people are generally too wise; we know too much of everything; are too busy with ourselves; and thereby make ourselves uneasy.

But a small, sick child lies down speechless and suffers; sometimes with a painful expression on the face, to be sure, but yet mostly as a background of that painful expression with charming childlike features.

To be a doctor of children therefore is something altogether different from being a doctor of grown people. Adults tell all sorts of things, what they have felt and experienced. They can answer every sort of question you may put. And afterward they can inform you about the several things, regarding which you gave them direction. But with a child this is not so.

A children's doctor can look at the suffering child,

feel his pulse, observe a few phenomena and try to guess something from the as yet little expressive features of the face, but that is all. All the rest must go upon intuition.

For, and this is the pathetic part of it, even when he is very sick, a child scarcely knows of his sickness. He has no thought about it. Passively he lets sickness come upon him. He feels indeed, that something strange is happening to him, but knows not what. All therefore you hear of a sick child is mostly a troubled exclamation of pain, as is told of the child of the Shunammite.

BUT for this very reason with a sick child belongs *his mother*. And it is a witness against the motherheart, when in such trying moments some one else understands better than the mother the sacred art, of ameliorating the suffering of that dear, suffering child and take away the trouble.

The mother is with the sick child the of God appointed nurse. Not that there are no others, oftentimes an older sister, able with great devotion to take care of the sick child; but because, especially in days of pain and sickness, there operates a mystery between a young child and the mother.

Also after the mother brought her little one into the world, there continues to operate a certain secret relation between her and the fruit of her womb. A relation, which is strongly felt at first, because she feeds the little one with her own milk. But which also still continues with the weaned child, and, as a rule, only begins to diminish when the child goes to school.

And that magnetic tie, if we may say so, which the mother feels binding her to her young child and the young child to his mother, operates at once so much more strongly, when the little one begins to suffer and becomes so ill, that he must die.

Then that mother *comforts* that little child, even though she does nothing else than sit quietly by his side. Then that intuitively appropriated motherlove imparts rest to the suffering child. It quiets his pain. And if he must die, it eases the death struggle.

AND, by the very working of that mysterious power the sick-bed of a child as a rule is so much more beautiful than the sick-bed of an adult.

Of course there are exceptions. Sometimes you find a crib with a very fretful child, which is troublesome and naughty; and over against this a bed, on which a pious child of God has waited more than fifty years for his Lord and Savior in holy peace.

But these are exceptions, and, as a rule, the sick-bed of our little ones is so much richer, so long as you but understand the art, of reading in that quiet and silent suffering what expresses itself therein.

With a young child there is no struggling against what God brings upon him. Just because a young child knows so much less, he makes so much easier a surrender of himself.

Also a little child lives for the most part in that naïve faith, which indeed without more is not saving, but yet comes so much nearer to the piety of the Sermon

on the Mount, than much wisdom, which we older ones
have to narrate.

When Jesus speaks of not being careful for the
morrow, but to live like the birds and the flowers, that
live from God's hand and are so gloriously cared for
by God, does not such a sick child seem, far more than
the sick of later years, like the lilies of the field and
the birds of the air, of which Jesus preached so touchingly and with such emphasis?

Yea, when you see Jesus take a little child and
place it in the midst of strong, big men, that were His
disciples, and then hear Him say, that they must become
as such a little child, does it not then for us elders also
apply to the sick-bed, that our sick-bed is God-glorifying
only, when upon our sick-bed also we have become as
the sick child on mother's lap?

A child that is sick, does not lose himself in his
sickness.

Call to mind for a moment, that a sick child, as
soon as he has a moment of relief, is at once inclined
again to play, or to listen to an interesting story, and
resume again his dear little face as of old.

A child has no knowledge yet of melancholy. He
does not concentrate all his thinking and deliberating
upon his sickness. He does not demur nor complain;
neither is he so fretful as sick folks of years frequently
are.

And, naturally, this is easy for a child, for his
world is still small, he has nothing to care for yet, he
does not look upon life so inquisitively and surmisingly,
and has never yet had any thought about the mystery of
suffering.

But by reason of this there is alive on the bottom

of the childheart a quieter and richer confidence in his
Father Who is in the heavens. He is not plagued as yet
by much reasoning, and therefore lives more in concrete
representations, just as the Bible continuously tries to
impress it upon us elders. Representations of a Father-
house above, and a God Who lives there, and looks down
upon us, and thinks of us, and lets His angels keep invisible watch, and in case we die, awaits us above.

And however childlike-naïve all this may live in
the imagination of that dear, suffering child, might not
that youthful little soul therefore often be nearer to the
truth and the reality, than the reverie and murmuring
of those aged of days, who reason, O, so wisely, about
their sickness and about their dying?

With such a young child it always is, as though on
the background you observe the presence of God and
His angels, while of this sacred loveliness so frequently
with the aged of days you find nothing.

MANY have no eye for this, and therefore learn nothing
from such a sick-bed of a child; any more than they ever
learn to understand of the quiet preachment, that comes
to them from the world of children.

Yet a Christian may not do so.

For this our Savior has pointed us far too frequently to the child life and to the child world: not
merely that we should carry on our heart the training of
these little ones, but also that we should let ourselves be
trained by them.

He who does not love children, has herein a witness against his *heart*, and we add thereto against his

*faith.* Yea, we would almost doubt whether one can stand as child right before God, if he has not first learned from little children what it is to be a child.

But though it is true, what we by no means deny, that by much troublesomeness and all sorts of naughtinesses, as in the fullness of life they run and romp, children frequently repel, in sickness this becomes so altogether different.

Then that sinfulness in our childen for so large a part falls away. Then something so sacred draws about them.

And therefore the little child, especially upon the sick-bed, is to us so glorious a witness to what, in distress and death, by a *childlike* faith, can also be our part.

## XIII

## *"She Had Hard Labor"*

### HARD IN HER LABOR

To become mother is the richest wealth, that is allowed by God to the woman's heart, but *this rose-branch also has its thorns*. What in Paradise God pronounced upon Eve, that she would bring forth her child in sorrow, has after her been the lot of every woman born of a woman. No childbirth without anguish.

It is indeed entirely true, that the suffering during and the after-pains after this anguish is not on a line *with sickness*. There is no poisonous corruption here at play. No medicine is administered against it. Even though it can bring a precious life into danger, of itself it does not lead to death, but to life. Sickness, unless there is an antidote, goes through suffering into death. Childbirth, provided circumstances are not untoward, goes from suffering to resurrection and renewal of life.

But though there is no sickness in the mystery of childbirth by itself, yet you cannot say, that it is natural. *Un*natural, *anti*natural rather, says the Scripture, is this rise of the new life from the sometimes so dreadful menacing ordeal and the sometimes death-shore approaching agony.

No, says God's Word, so it was *not* ordained by your God. In His creation, had it not been disturbed by sin, the new, young life would have come into being from pure delight, in sweet sensation, without aught suggestive of pain.

That now it is, as it is, God Himself in Paradise explains to be a *punishment*. A bitter punishment not imposed upon the man, but upon the woman, in connection with what the Scripture declares: "And Adam was not deceived, but the woman being deceived was in the transgression" (I Tim. 2, 14).

And it is true, indeed, that not every woman has a like part in this anguish. The dispensation here is indeed very unequal. For one almost without suffering all the months that precede, just a painful emotion for a short time, and then, after speedy recovery, a picture of health and strength. And over against this so many another woman, who is almost exhausted by reason of all sorts of vexations, before she comes to her hour, in that hour itself sometimes to be tortured as on a rack; and after that terrible hour to suffer for weeks and months together, in case she recovers at all; and even if she does, to mourn all her life long the aftermath of that awful hour in broken strength that is never restored.

In between these extremes, of which one, as is said, does not turn a hand for it, and the other who had to pay for it worse than with her life, there are hundreds and thousands, whose lot changes with lesser and greater difference.

But however great the difference, woman *as woman* continues to bear this bitter suffering. And how this suffering is to be divided among the daughters of her generation, is not subject to human decision. That decides, that divides and appoints He, Who can make no mistake, the Lord our God.

PRUDISHNESS in our times banishes everything connected with childbirth from conversation.

Pure, exalted, free exchange of thought regarding this important chapter of our human life is smothered, that, alas, all too frequently, the impure and unholy whisper of sinful passion may be put in its place.

Our Savior does not put His seal to this prudery. Openly, in the hearing of the multitudes, before the ear of His disciples, He recalls these hidden, deep mysteries of human life.

"A woman, when she is in travail, hath sorrow," so He spake in S. John 16, 21, "because her hour is come; but as soon as she is delivered of the child, she remembereth no more the anguish, for joy that a man is born into the world."

And so it is, praise be to God, also in by far most instances. Truly weakening sensations months before, and also bitter anguish in the birththroes, but, when it has been endured, heavenly gladness in the blessed mothereye, when for the first time it may look upon the little one, that drinks in milk at her breast.

Motherwealth after motheranguish.

And yet, this is no fixed rule.

Sometimes in that anxious hour the mother or the little one succumbed. At rare times even mother and child together.

Then in one moment of time there is the ruin of a hope, so sweetly cherished for months together. Then there is death among people, where new life was about to be given. Everything somber, closing up the heart, and instead of the little baby voice, that was to be heavenly music, nothing but sobs and tears.

A young mother, who after everything that has been

struggled through and endured, finds nothing but a cold, white infant-corpse, that mainly from love is concealed from her.

Or again, the baby saved, but the mother succumbed, and the newly born infant *without mother* come into the world.

And sometimes the saddest of all.

A husband who loved, a young man who for months already had dreamed himself a father, and now . . . *nothing more.* No child he had prayed for, and no more wife, who would have given him that child.

Nothing, nothing but black night, till the God of all comfort comes to his soul and calls out unto him: "In your blood, in the blood of your soul, live" (Ezek. 16, 9).

YET, though it runs no such tragic course, childbirth ever remains an episode of extreme importance in the homelife, which as a general thing is treated with greatest superficiality.

For indeed the cradle may interest you, and the beautiful infant, as one of God's little creatures, may lead you up to the Creator of the children of men. It is even human, and therefore good, that all there is charming about it, because it is small and lovely, attracts you; and that the nurse and all that goes with her name, engages you.

But yet, shall it be well, then here also life must be lived *more deeply*.

More deeply lived by the husband, who, though the wife bears the anguish, yea, just because the wife bears the anguish, in holy sympathy of love, will suffer with her whom he loves. If ever the heart of a man is drawn out from his selfishness, to forget himself and to give himself to another, it must be in those days of anxiety.

But the young mother also must multiply thoughts within herself, and live through days of so high seriousness, seriously also with respect to the future.

Only by becoming a mother, the young woman breaks forever with a life, that in many ways was merely play with her.

All this is now ended, and brought to nought. Now calling beckons; from now on there awaits her a glorious task, to train that little child, given her of God, first for the family, then for the world, and under it all, for heaven.

Also the *motherbreast*, undoubtedly, for that too is a miracle of God in your own blood; but more still your *motherheart* is what your baby asks for, or better yet, God asks it in behalf of the darling, which He gave you.


A second, a third childbirth does not bring that anxiety and neither has it therefore that great charm; and yet, unto the end, no course through the mystery of life remains so deeply serious.

You would say, there is but one way through this hiddenness; and see, in the end every new confinement proves to be different. Never the same, always different, be it the impressions of the heart, be it by what God had appointed for us in it.

But what above all imparts so different a character

to a second or third confinement, is the little one you already had.

For the first time that little sister and brother in your own family. Something you well knew in your parental home, when you yourself were a little brother or little sister, but had never so enjoyed it in its beautiful poetry.

That little darling at the cradle of the newly born. Understanding nothing of it, and yet in his childlike way gazing so seriously at the little wight. O, so beautiful, and yet also again so bitter; for almost never have two little children been seen in one home, but early or late, there sprang up a fountain of that selfsame water, that once poisoned all Cain's heart and made him seek so terrible a relaxation in Abel's death.

O, from that chamber of birth are the issues of life, and he who has but an eye for it, observes sometimes already in that chamber a whole world in miniature.

WHAT is most serious therefore remains: A childbirth *lived through without God*.

This truly is the zenith of self-delusion. For how could there ever be a childbirth, if there were no God; if God did not create; and did not give the wife the motherblessing to bring forth.

A mother and a child do not yet make a childbed. In the chamber of birth God must always be present to you. That only imparts to it a sacred mystery, and so only can also the suffering, the sometimes bitter anguish, in confident faith be struggled through.

Then, before it comes so far, *prayer* is made. Prayer, before hope came, that hope might come, and when it came, that it might be fulfilled. In and during the fulfillment, prayer for assistance and help. And prayer the first evening after the birth for the life of the young baby.

So prayer is made and thanks given. For God is good and great, and a God full of compassion also to that little child.

Does not Baptism already beckon?

And Baptism, that holy Baptism of God Triune, what else does it say, than that your little one, yea, truly is yours, but yet really already from his birth belongs to his Father Who is in heaven?

## XIV

# *"Evil That Brings Disease"*

### SICKNESS AND SIN

In Paradise, as you instinctively accept, sickness and disease would have been as unthinkable, as bodily anguish or pain. Your Jesus, during his sojourn on earth among us, lying sick in bed, is a thought, which you cannot connect with His Name. And that upon the new earth, when the glory of the Lord shall penetrate all things, there will still be doctors, to minister to us their medicine, is to you a *contradiction in terms*, an idea that contradicts itself.

With deeper insight therefore you must of yourself come to the conclusion, which Holy Scripture presents to you, and acknowledge, that all sickness and all pain hang together with the sad fact, that sin hides in our heart, and that all we together are a sinful race.

Without sin no death; but when you sin, though it be but once, death comes surely and certainly, then you *must* die the death.

Without sin, nothing comes down to this earth but Divine blessing; but after the first sin it reads at once: Cursed is the ground for thy sake, and anguish shall pursue you even in bringing forth children.

All sickness, all pain is a sign of that selfsame destructive power, which once is consummated in your dying.

And therefore it is not enough to acknowledge, that your dying is related to sin.

In like relation to sin stands likewise both *sickness* and *pain*.

Not, of course, as though it can be said of every attack of pain or disease, that it came upon you by reason of this definite sin or because of that unrighteousness.

What you have to confess, is, that by sin, curse and death came into the world and upon our race, and that by reason of this you also can have no pain or be sick, except as you undergo a part of the suffering that came upon our race, for the sake of the selfsame sin, for which you too are responsible; wherewith you yourself have been in league; yea, of which you carry about with you the seeds in your own heart.

SOMETIMES this is directly evident, as when by intemperance a man has incurred sickness, or by carelessness has jeopardized his health, not to say anything of those dreadful diseases, which follow in the wake of the sin of drink and lewdness.

But these are exceptions.

Generally the relation between sickness and sin lies *not* so clearly bare. It is truly there, but it is hidden.

But that it is there, you observe with great pestilences, when the conscience in general is terror stricken, and thousands upon thousands, who had scarcely any thought of God, at once become troubled by reason of their sin.

You see this with diseases as Miriam's leprosy,

of which it is expressly said, that it came upon her as a plague and punishment.

And you also see it, as often as with healing of disease Jesus pronounced absolution, saying: "Thy sins are forgiven thee."

And do you ask for proof from the present, then observe, that they, who have tenderest knowledge of their own heart, even in ordinary sicknesses feel themselves pricked in the conscience and thirst for atonement, while unspiritual and superficial persons on their sick-bed drowse without spiritual concern.

YET it is important, that this relation between sickness and sin be more closely observed.

Not to say, that a healthy man is virtuous, and that one, who is much troubled with poor health, must be a sinner in the dark.

Leave that false application of Job's erring friends, and think of the saying of Jesus regarding the man born blind, that that blindness was no punishment for what he or his father had misdone, but an affliction, from which the glorifying of God's Name had to ripen.

This personal application does not become you, except God makes it in your own conscience.

But just as little does it become you to say, that there never is a causal relation between the transgression of God's command and a sickly affection in your constitution.

The apostle wrote so positively to the church at Corinth (I, 11, 30), that in the Lord's Supper they desecrated God's covenant, and "that for this cause many among them were weak and sickly and some had already died."

And this same relation, which the apostle thus establishes between spiritual transgression and external suffering, was already known to Solomon.

He too wrote, that the feeling of envy, inward spite and anger, with which all sorts of experience in financial concerns sometimes fill our heart, *"is an evil that brings on disease"* (Prov. 14, 30).

Also your doctors tell you, that there are all sorts of indispositions, which find their origin in reveries and unhealthy humors of your inner being.

By inworking upon the soul to heal the body, is sometimes the intention, on which they act.

With the insane they seek through the body to work upon the soul, but with these ruffled persons through the soul upon the body.

And in both lies the acknowledgment, that from the tie that binds soul and body together, there arises also a certain relation between sin and sickness.

INVESTIGATIONS in this domain are still of little significance and their result extremely meager; but it is acknowledged that here is a wealth of knowledge, that can become of high significance for the healing of our sick.

At present microbe and bacillus draw almost all attention. But suppose, that indeed in this form we were on the track of the general nature of all disease, the end would not be reached. For there still follows the second inquiry: Whence those microbes? Whence has one this, the other that power? How do they come so suddenly,

presently to disappear again? What do they owe their
presence to? And above all how do they stand in connection with a man's person?

If all sickness and death are by reason of sin, you
cannot rest, before the common root of all sickness is
traced to sin. An investigation in which perhaps we
shall never succeed, but which yet should not be neglected.

That by giving vent to his passion, a man can incur
a shock, that costs him his life, has been all but too
frequently witnessed.

No one indeed denies this.

But the question is, whether there is not some
deeper lying relation also, where most people do not
look for it.

To come back to that irascible, passionate man—has
not such an hothead by indulgence in his passion, instead of curbing the same, aggravated the evil in his
blood that irritated him?

With a passionate man there is something in his
blood, that the slow of spirit lacks. Now that evil something in his blood can be fed or starved. Starved by
self-control, or fed by indulging passion. And when for
years together a man yields to this, and so feeds the
evil in his blood, is it then not plain, that in the end the
blood becomes too much for him, and ends in a stroke,
and costs him his life?

Do not pent-up envy and rancor, have an equally
deleterious effect upon our constitution?

The Lord forbids you to hate any man. You shall

forgive your brother seventy times seven, and love your enemy, and bless them that curse you.

Now do this, do it honestly, do it with all your heart, and a glad, cheerful sense of victory comes over you, and the blood streams vigorously through your veins. But also, ignore this positive command of your Savior, so that the sun sets upon your wrath, and you go on carrying about with you malicious envy and rancor in your heart against all sorts of persons, yea, that you live in enmity sometimes with brothers, then of course that envy and that anger and that evil rancor poisons your blood; your heart shrinks, your inner equability is disturbed, and presently in all sorts of indisposition and sickness becomes evident the fatal result of your loveless existence.

So people who always sit gazing upon their money. They are always busy with that money. At home, at their work, on the way, even on their bed. It is always one concentration of their heart and their person upon this one point. And of course their whole personal existence suffers under it. And that in turn affects their constitution.

How irregularity of life destroys health and strength, needs no reminder. Such people are like a clock, the hands of which one turns every time again some hours backwards and then again forwards, till finally by this irregularity the clock gives out.

How melancholy, i.e., evil somberness and atrabiliousness has destroyed treasures of courage and joy of life, we still see time and time again on every hand; and, of course, also that melancholy is *sin*. A sin, that one first indulges in, till at length he is no more able to struggle against it, and of which one becomes a victim.

O, the soul works in so many ways upon our frail and tender body.

And this you should consider, not, of course, that you might say: "Then I will fight against that sin, to protect my body," as though otherwise that sin could be tolerated, but for the sake of your health must be avoided.

No, but that with slow and with acute sickness every one may learn to enter in upon himself, in God's presence to ask himself: Is there indeed direct connection?

## XV

# "Consume Away Like a Moth"

### PINING AWAY

"WHEN Thou with rebukes dost chasten man," says David, "thou makest his beauty to consume away like a moth. Surely every man is vanity!" (Psalm 39, 12.)

David could speak thus, because evidently He had been much sick. Nowhere more than in the Psalms you find continual references to all sorts of sickness. Sometimes it is even almost possible to make out the nature of David's sickness from this or another Psalm. As for instance from Psalm 38, from which it is evident how near unto death David had been.

It is customary indeed to take many of these utterances of soul in a spiritual sense; something that by reason of the coherence between soul and body is permissible; yet it behooves us first to ask what David immediately meant.

By so doing, the sick-bed also would find its place more often in the preaching of the Word, and with visiting the sick the Minister of the Word would observe, how greatly his language, his speech and his provision of sacred direction and comforting would be enriched.

Sickness is such a weighty element in the homelife, and also in the faithlife of God's children, when this broad domain, in which so much anguish and so much anxiety is suffered, is excluded from the sacred.

Yea, one may say, that a considerable part of the

purpose, for which God the Lord sends us all sorts of
sickness, is altogether lost, when by reason of carelessness or by overspirituality, the rich teaching of the Word
regarding the sick-bed does not come to its own.

CONSIDER for a moment, therefore, what the Psalmist
says of the rapid exhaustion of strength, which with so
many an ailment overtakes the sufferer.

*Then consumes,* says David, *our beauty like a moth.*
Or rather, for in this also the Lord God is the worker,
then He *makes* our beauty to consume away like a moth.

You see this especially with one who is still in the
strength of his life. Then there was first thriving, sometimes glowing health. Muscles, that could hold out.
Strong pulsebeat in the blood. A fresh and animated
exterior. An eye, that by its glistening addressed
you.

But scarcely began the germ of sickness to develop
itself and the disease to take hold, but the strength broke,
the muscles became flabby, the eye duller, weaker the
voice, and everything that only lately was all animation
and buoyancy, is suddenly gone.

When you come to the bedside, and have not
watched the transition from day to day, you scarcely
recognize the sufferer.

Everything is so changed.

It is sometimes said: melted like snow before the
sun; but the Psalmist uses a yet more striking figure.

Like as you catch a moth, and rub him in pieces
between your fingers, so that you scarcely know, what
becomes of him, so likewise consumes that beauty and

that virile strength, which before the sickness so attracted you.

THEN he who suffers and they that are at the bedside learn, that surely every man is vanity.

In ordinary times we know two kinds of people. Strong and weak. And we suffer with the weak, because we realize how difficult to them every step is, which they take on the highway of life. But with the strong we receive rather the impression of strength, as though ordinary human vanity were not *their* portion. One laughs at them, when they complain. And spoiled by that feeling of strength and by that mocking laugh, they all too readily imagine, that for them there is less need, every morning and every evening anew to pray for well-being to the God of their life.

But in the sick-room this difference is gone.

Then the strong man, too, has become mortally weak, and it even seems that the dreadful transition from strength to exhaustion, brings out the more the weakness of the strong.

Then one sees how it took almost nothing, to cast down that strong man like an helpless child.

Surely, as David says, *every* man is vanity.

David himself undoubtedly was a strong, powerful man, and yet he had experienced himself, how as in one moment God had turned him into a trembling soul, him, who once like an oak of the forest had aroused the jealousy of many.

THEN with rebukes the Lord chastens man for sin, says David.

Not of course as though he who remained in health, had not sinned, and as though he who became ill, had fallen into special sin.

This they who care for the sick know better, and the good nurse at least is always more troubled about her own sin than about the sin of her who lies so mortally ill.

Serious illness always speaks to the conscience of those who stand about the bed.

But therefore it must never be forgotten, that *without sin* there would have been neither sickness nor mortal anxiety.

All sickness is prelude to death, and is there solely on account of sin.

But that chastening of sickness does not count individually, does not go head for head, and is not measured out man for man after the measure of every one's sin.

This chastening comes upon all; it is poured out upon the masses, and God portions out sickness according to His divine counsel, that not only our own, but also the sickness of others, should strike and humble us.

Sickness is common suffering, which is most unequally divided, whereby God instructs us, that we do not only have our personal sin, but also our collective sin, and that not least *against this* His holiness is in wrath. O, if there were no sickness, how much more over-bold man would be.

And also how much love and how much devotion, which are in evidence now, would never have unfolded.

YET the main preaching of such consuming of the strength of the sufferer is *our vanity*.

Not least in days of such anxiety must the lesson of our *dependence* be learned.

Of deep dependence *with* and *without* medicine.

He who calls upon God only, when there is no cure, does not understand the highness of the Lord, and under-values the comfort, which He, and He alone, gave us in medicine.

O, it is so absurd, at every meal you take, to invoke God's blessing, and to have no need of that blessing, when our life hangs on a silken thread, and medicine is all we can take.

But that lesson of our deep dependence must not be limited to the sick-room.

The purpose of your sickness is not, that for some months you should depend upon God, and presently, when your breath is able again to move a feather, to forget your God again.

It is a lesson *for life*, which must be learned in the sick-room.

One who has recovered from sickness should never be able again to forget his deep dependence upon his God. And they who stood around his bed should have learned by watching him, how absolutely nothing they also are without their God.

After sickness the faith of God's child must work an effect of its own.

Surely not to murmur and not to complain too much; but also and no less, to learn better than other-wise could have been learned that difficult lesson, that everything is *vanity*, and that he alone who rests in God's hand, has peace within.

## XVI

# "A Testament Is of Force After Men Are Dead"

## YOUR TESTAMENT

In every testament as such lies the confession of an eternal life; the acknowledgment that he who died still is; and that also after his death his will binds those that remained behind.

Had not our human race for centuries lived in the sure confidence, that also after death our existence goes on, the idea of making a testament or of respect for a testament would never have come to any one (Heb. 9, 17).

Then a testament has no sense.

Then respect for the will of the deceased regarding the disposition of his goods, which is so indispensable for the validity of every testament, would be altogether wanting.

One would act as though the dead no more existed; would have no regard for what he willed or did not will; and consider what he left behind no more as an *inheritance*, but as a property that had become *ownerless*, and could be appropriated.

Now, on the other hand, when after one's death his testament is opened, and the members of the family gather around that testament, the sense expresses itself by this, that he who died, as it were after his death, is still in their midst, and now by means of this testament makes known to them his will.

Could it actually be, that, momentarily, the deceased returned in the midst of his own, his word would be listened to with respect and reverence; the disposition of his will would count for all as law; and of resistance there would be no mention.

But since this is not possible, the testament fulfills the selfsame sacred task; it is for this reason, that the reading of a testament in the presence of all concerned is a moment of such solemnity; and that on the part of government such a far-reaching power of disposition is attributed to the testament.

FROM this it follows of itself, that also the making of his testament postulates faith in eternity.

Thoughtlessly to find one's way to the notary and make one's testament, is contrary to the nature of this transaction.

He who is to make his testament, must be seriously-minded. This does not mean that he must have a long and solemn face; for all affectation is abomination to the Lord. To be "seriously-minded" means: that you do not come to an act like this without careful forethought, and due consideration of all the pros and cons, and are deeply sensible of the responsibility, which by this action comes to rest upon you.

Rightly to make one's testament, one must really imagine himself in the condition of being dead, and of appearing after death once more in the midst of his own, to make his last will known to them. And as one would then speak, so he must now write it down in his testament.

Our fathers therefore had the fixed habit, to begin every testament with an invocation of God Triune. Making a testament was looked upon as a deed done in the presence of God. The last act of stewardship. Or at least a responsibility, from which of itself that last act was to be born.

It was even frequently the custom, before the testament was made, to call upon God Almighty in prayer, that by His mindful making Spirit He would give direction, that everything might be well ordered and nothing be forgotten.

So almost every testament in time past bore a pious or at least a serious character.

One wrote it himself. One expressed himself in it. The one this way, the other that. And thereby such a testament had also personal value.

ALL this also, however, has become different.

Our present-day testaments no longer know the Lord of life and death. They are almost exclusively *material* testaments. They deal with money and again money. And when one leaves no money to any one, who then asks about his testament?

Hence accuracy in the make-up of a testament is now the main concern, for which reason it is mostly not only *written* by the lawyer, but also *composed,* so that one himself does nothing, except put his name under it.

O, from nothing more than from the style and form of testaments is the character of an age known.

Consult ten, twenty testaments of the sixteenth and

seventeenth centuries, and everything tells you at once, that you have to do with a generation that fears God. But examine ten, twenty testaments now, and in everything you observe, that in our nineteenth century god Mammon has pretty well made the spirit of men to wither.

They are all testaments after a fixed model, and of the person, whose testament it is, you learn nothing.

He does not speak, he does not express himself.

You learn nothing of his character.

Fortunate that at least we still have the holographical testaments.

Therein at least something still speaks, and, properly sealed, they are placed with the notary, without the notary knowing anything it contains.

ONLY in one point the pious, discreet spirit of our fathers is not altogether gone, namely, in making bequests of a part of one's property to what among the things of God's kingdom, among relatives, or among the poor is in need of financial assistance.

This also became less frequent, and it is incomprehensible how rich Christian millionaires could prove so parsimonious. Nevertheless bequests are made. Papers make mention of it again and again. Sometimes even very large sums. Only recently a devout Minister of the Word went to his reward, who had made disposition of his entire property, five hundred thousand guilders, in this godly manner.

And herein at least speaks the heart.

In such a testament this indicates the person.

From this, at least, one learns, in what direction his spirit moved and what the institutions were of his love.

And yet let us not boast too much of this in our age.

For in our age money has been made like water, and it is generally estimated that since 1830 in most of the states of Europe wealth has more than doubled.

And after that standard the sum of legacies is by no means what it ought to be. So little, indeed, that the increase in capital of institutions kept no equal pace even by far with the increase of population.

For not merely *wealth*, but also the population has more than doubled, and this is not thought of, and so counted we fall great sums behind.

Especially burghers who became rich were very delinquent in this, and while over against their increased wealth there was a dreadful increase in poverty and need, it can by no means be said that one has tried, at least after his death, to care for these more general interests.

Even among Christians many a one died, who left wealth behind, had no children to provide for, and yet fell altogether short in his care for this general need.

THIS does not say that all former dispositions were of pure alloy.

Liberal legacies to church or poor of olden times spoke oftentimes of much sin.

And so there was many a man, who after a life in sin and wantonness, thought he could buy for his soul a safe retreat in heaven, by leaving much of his money for sacred purposes.

It especially came to pass, that he who had made money in an unrighteous way, made agreement with his conscience, first to enjoy during his lifetime what he could, and then to make good his unrighteous dealings and robberies, by giving it to the church at his death.

And, of course, this is no standpoint pleasing to God.

But this does not give our age the right to look down upon this from the height.

Even now the capitals that have been laid up by craftiness, abuse of power, speculation and gambling, are legion, and when in the face of this even that single waking of the conscience remains wanting, which at least in dying desires to undo the wrong, are you then not put to shame by the Middle Ages?

What alone also in this can bring betterment is the working out of faith.

Also your testament must be *from faith*; otherwise it is sin.

From faith: That your goods are God's property, and that you are nothing but a steward over them, and thus as steward owe your Lord an account.

So comes the testament into relation with the last judgment; for if of anything, of your testament you shall give account to God.

And now it is granted, that for the making of such a sound testament one must have come to certain years. To the years in which, in the ordinary course of life, one sees his end approaching. But the rule, that our years are sixty and seventy years, may never be crossed.

Also in our civil law there must more and more be insisted upon a manner of making one's testament, which harmonizes with the sacred character of the same.

And what indeed were to be wished for our Christian people, is, that in city and country town, on every hand, notaries were given us, who practiced also this part of their calling as in the holy presence of God.

A more free office of notary would be a blessing to our Christian people.

## XVII

## *"Seek Ye the Lord, While He May Be Found"*

### SICK-BED CONVERSION

You cannot say, that the Lord your God is always equally near to you. There is sometimes so much doing in the daily life, in the house, in trade and calling, that amidst all this activity at most a single hasty thought of God can pass through your soul, and little more than what Luther called an "ejaculatory prayer" can ascend from your soul to the Lord.

Opportunity and calling are so different with respect to this. A woman, with but one little child in a quiet family, has so much freer access than a mother, who, unable to engage help, has to get along alone with five or six young children. Also the farmer, who by himself alone labors in the field, has so much more chance in life to be busy with his God, than, for instance, a bus conductor, who from early morning till late night is in the midst of distraction.

And God the Lord knows this; for His is the disposition of our life, and in His judgment upon our persons all this counts.

But what shall never be excused in you, is that you treat with negligence those special times and opportunities, which your God gives you to seek Him. And among these opportunities are the times when you are sick.

Not when you lie delirious or are overpowered by

cutting pain, but when sickness or accident temporarily renders you unable to work, and shut out from all activity, you are confined to your sick-room, or lie down upon your sick-bed.

Those are days of retirement for you, when the Lord calls you to His hidden tent. When everything about you is still, and therefore He, the Lord, can speak to you. That thoughts multiply themselves in you, and thought can center itself so undisturbedly upon the Eternal Being.

That is the findingtime, and renders Isaiah's word valid for you: "Seek ye the Lord, while He may be found, call ye upon him while he is near" (Isaiah 55, 6).

Not as though your sick-room exclusively afforded you that "findingtime." God is rich and has a thousand other occasions, to let Himself be found of you. Sometimes amidst a howling storm, with a shipwreck that menaces your life, far stronger than amidst the stillness, which your sickness offers.

Even as on Sinai your God can be in the storm and in the fire. Only, He can also, as with Elijah, come in the still small voice.

And the object of our word with your own conscience is reached, when you acknowledge, that the sick-room also or the sick-bed brings you a call from God, and this call in you tells you, that your God can be found of you, and that therefore you must seek Him.

And there is so much, that helps us in this.

Nothing that diverts you, and so much that leads you upward.

You are then no longer the strong and healthy one, who were sufficient unto yourself, but you feel yourself broken in strength, reminded of your weakness, and placed in your dependence before the Lord.

Even when your sickness bears no serious character, so that there is no question about any danger for your life, yet all sickness takes away the false notion, as though you possessed strength in yourself.

And this favors the attitude of mind, that is necessary to turn yourself to your God. To Him in Whose hand your life is, Who alone is able to bless the medicine ministered unto you, and Who, when sickness abates, is the alone Mighty One, to restore your strength of life to you and the refreshing feeling of being well again.

A sick-bed, lived through without God, is therefore the gambling away of a grace offered unto you.

The letting go for lost of an opportunity, of meeting your God, that perhaps never returns.

Your God *was* then to be found, and see, you have not sought Him. He *was* near, and you have not called upon Him.


But, thank God, it is not always so.

There are also those, and they are not few, who may glory, that in the days of their illness the hiddenness of the Lord was conscious reality to them. That God was near and that they called upon Him; that He was to be found and that they sought Him, and were able to carry away from their sick-bed as ripe fruit of the soul a prayerful fellowship with the Eternal Being.

Yea, that after recovery, they surely thanked Him also for having raised them up again, but more ardently and with greater heartfeltness praised Him and jubilated over what God had done to their soul.

So it was a sickness not unto death and also not merely unto recovery, but to a glorifying of God's Name and to an enriching of their inner wealth of salvation.

Something that is said not only of the few, to whom the sick-bed in God's hand was the means of bringing them to a first conversion and a first jubilation of faith; but also, and still much more of them, who had already drunk something of the Fountain of Life, but with whom the real, the consuming thirst after the water of life had never yet been quickened.

Yea, one can say even yet more. The sick-bed has often been a blessing not alone to the sick himself, but equally often to those who were in the same house with the sick, to them who cared for him, who watched by his bedside, whether it was anxiety that moved the heart, or the alarm in the house that compelled deeper seriousness of thought.

O, you do not know, what spiritual blessings go for lost in hospitals and asylums, except they are institutions, where the Mediator is confessed, and the tone of the house and the spirit of the whole social atmosphere leads up to that Only One, Who can protect us.

*Seek Him*, so sounds the prophetcall, while He is to be found; and that seeking of the living God is so deeply significant.

Certain interest in eternal things is not enough;

also living life along with your church is not enough; and equally little, being busy with the Word.

All this is thinkable and possible, and occurs even frequently, apart from any reality of a genuine seeking after the living God.

One then knew much of God, and read much of the Holy One of Israel, and was zealous for His Name, and was troubled about one's soul, and reached out the hand after the eternal inheritance, but deepfelt longing of soul did not as yet go out after the God of life.

It was not yet what David exclaimed: "As the hart panteth after the water brooks, so panteth my soul after thee, O God!"

And yet to that seeking itself it must come, for where is otherwise that *love*, which must be the sweetness of the soul; and the apostle so definitely declares, that it is nothing else yet but sounding brass and a tinkling cymbal, while you may be ever so rich in all gifts of grace, but are still stranger to the mystery of blessed love.

"I love, for the Lord hears me," is the cry of a soul, that thirsted after the living God, was no more able to go without Him, and at length obtained answer to her call, and in becoming aware of that hidden fellowship, feels so irresistibly the tingling of holiest love, the love of her God.


AND it is true, indeed, that after sickness the days of convalescence disappoint again.

When presently strength returns in the blood, and the pulsebeat is stronger again, and we go back to our busy, active life with all its diversions, all its temptations and all its distractions, the sobering is often very trying and sometimes it seems, that all the blessed experience of the sick-bed was nothing but self-deception, so far do we then at times wander away again from our God.

Yea, he who is not on his guard, can after his recovery sometimes almost lose everything that he gained. For on the sick-bed, in solitariness, amidst the stillness to seek God, is so much easier than to stay near by God, and to keep God close by, in the midst of exhausting activity.

But yet, when spiritual direction is not wanting, and friends and members of the family, and above all, office-bearers in the church understand their duty, the soul is duly warned against this danger.

And though it is then easy to understand, that for a time again clouds gather between our God and our soul, also that first barrenness and darkness pass away again.

God knows His own, of whom He has been found, and He seeks them out again and comes to sup with them.

And when that struggle too is ended, and in that struggle also victory is won, then come the still more happy and still more wealthy days, when our soul enjoys the fellowship with the Eternal Being, not only when the world has been shut out from us, but also in the midst of the roaring of its waves, when in the midst of the storm of life He commands stillness.

## XVIII

# "Thou Hast Turned for Me My Mourning Into Dancing"

### RECOVERED AGAIN

NOT every sickness is unto death. It even happens frequently in very serious illness, that the fear of death took hold of us and the thread of our life was almost cut, and prayer and supplication were heard and life was given back again.

But, alas, it is then that so often the *spiritual* fruit, which was hoped for both on behalf of the sick himself and of his family, remains wanting.

You would say: That will be just the other way. When God the Lord takes from us one of our most beloved treasures, there will be murmuring in the heart, and for awhile at least there will be an estrangement in the love, wherewith we have loved our God. But when the blow does *not* fall, and in the hour of gravest danger God comes to your help, so that your sick revives again, O, then it will all be one song of praise and jubilation. Love and praise as offerings laid on the altar of the Lord.

And yet, experience teaches otherwise.

When it goes into death, yea, then the heart is deeply moved; then it is as though for a moment the world loses all charm for us; and as though we sensed more truly than ever, where our real native land is. Not here, but up yonder.

Almost at no time more than in days of fresh

mourning is there remembrance of the Lord our God in our heart, upon our bed, in our conversation; and rarely does our prayer obtain a tenderer tone, than in just such a state of anguish of soul.

At the grave one can still say, that the high God receives *something* of His honor.

But when God did not slay, but lifted up again, and with our sick it went not unto death, but the Lord raised him up again from the sick-bed, *how is it then?*

And, alas, the answer to this question cannot be otherwise, than painful.

Ever and always yet in the tone of what Jesus said to the saved leper: "Were there not ten cleansed? Where are the nine? And are there none found that return, to give glory to God save this stranger?" (S. Luke 17, 17).

Was it better in bygone times?

Undoubtedly.

A sacred outpouring of heart as in Psalm 30 was interpreted on David's harp; a song of worship full of praise and thanksgiving as Hezekiah sang before his God; and so many other utterances, preserved for us in Scripture, bear abundant evidence of this.

And also in the ages, when in our country the church of God was flourishing, pious usages introduced the fixed rule, that in God's house not merely prayers were asked for the sick, but also thanksgivings were made for those whom God had raised up again.

Also thankofferings were almost a fixed rule, and that without there being any serious reason of complaint about a tendency toward workholiness.

And though we grant, that these outward signs seemed for a good part to float upon these usages, yet it is quite clear that such usage rather weakens the moment it ceases to be carried by a spirit of reality.

When no woman recovered from childbed goes out, except as her first going out is to go to church, openly to praise her God, by that church service, and by that thanksgiving, she experiences a feeling of thankfulness and an impulse to praise in the soul, which is honoring to God.

And that all this so largely fell away and passed into desuetude, is an evil omen.

O, we well know that there still remains *something*, and here and there even a great deal. In the country more than in the cities. Among the "common people" more than among gentlemen and ladies. After childbed more than after recovery from sickness. Very frequently there are thankofferings recorded for recoveries from illness, which bear witness to the generosity of many.

But all this does not silence our complaint.

There is retrogression in this public exhibition of thankfulness. And this retrogression in public expression of our gratitude betrays all too unmistakably that there is a slackening also in our heart; a slackening also in family life.

Now there is one circumstance, which bears mention if not by way of excuse with respect to this, yet at least by way of softening of judgment; we mean the sometimes so slow convalescence.

With death this is so altogether different. Then there is suddenly a fact that violently takes hold of one. Immediately after this follows mourning, care for the corpse, presently sad burial. So the ordinary course of life is broken. Everything works together to center your attention upon one point. You can almost think of nothing else. And so it takes no effort, with your heart and with your lips to be engaged in things eternal. Your dead himself beckons you.

But with convalescence all this is so different.

Yea, with some diseases there is what doctors call a crisis, so that there is a day of crisis, and on the evening of that day you feel, that now the balance was restored, and that God had brought deliverance.

But such is by no means the case with all convalescents.

With not a few it is a going up and down. Some better one day, and then less well the next. Especially in nervous cases, little can be said. Finally there is slow progress. But so slow and evasive, that from week to week, and from evening to morning, there is really nowhere a milepost by the way, of which you can say: "Up to this point death threatened, and from this point on I regained life."

Not seldom recovery itself, which comes at last, is even then so slow, that it takes days, weeks, months, before you come back to the former, ordinary life. Even then one feels so weak and so tired. The legs once so strong scarcely carry you. The head is still very sensitive. You can almost stand nothing, but it hurts you. You feel as though you have become a touch-me-not.

And as unobservedly as grass grows, so unobservedly you gain in strength, till at length you attempt to take up your work again. And so gradually you come back to the old life.

And, of course, at no point on the long way is there then one striking event, one single occurrence that makes an impression; nothing that snatches you away from your ordinary doings; and this is then so frequently the cause, that thanks do not rise in the heart, seek no utterance, and go out neither in praise nor in thank-offering.

THERE is need therefore of deep workings of faith, to have the honor of His Name come to God from a sick-bed that ends in recovery, more even than from a sick-bed that ends in death.

You would think that this would be otherwise; but yet this is not so.

When your God is gracious, and hears the supplications from your sick-bed, and lifts you up again, there is less probability that the honor of His Name is given Him, than when He remains deaf to your cry and lets you down into the pit.

But for this very reason among God's children sanctified attention must far more strongly than thus far be directed to this point.

They, who in earlier years had come to the gate of death, and called upon God, and were healed, and then made, O, so sacred a promise, only later on altogether to forget it, should turn in upon their inmost self and enter accusation against themselves about the lie in their heart. They should, as it were, in thought live over again anew their anxiety and their supplications, and so come to renewal of promise and renewal of vow, for the favor they enjoyed at God's hand.

That much for the past; but also for the present and the future, the seriousness of thanksgiving must waken again.

If you once know that slow recovery from sickness tends strongly to have you forget God's mercy, and withhold from Him your praise—and your thankoffering, when sickness comes, you will watch, pray, strive also against this. You will set yourself against it. And by intentional remembrance avert from you this sin of unthankfulness.

One will also assist the other in this matter. Father and mother will encourage in this, the child that recovered. Brother will wake up his friend. And he who prayed with him for deliverance, will afterward thank with him the God of his life.

FOR it must all end in the honor of God's Name, also our sickness and also our deliverance. The Lord has created all things and ever yet doeth all things, for His own Self's sake.

And therefore you sink in, and sink away from yourself, when from your life also that honor of His Name does not come to your God.

And if you say that it is almost impossible to remember just when you felt yourself altogether restored; well, then, come back to the ancient custom and see how wisely the church introduced that good custom, and appoint a day, on which with all your family you go to the house of God, in the midst of the congregation to sing praises and to offer your thanksgiving unto Him.

Just because convalescence takes so slow a course, appointing of such a day is so good.

Then there is a fixed point. Then there is a day on which all your thoughts can go back to what was suffered, to what love did to sustain you, to what was prayed and supplicated that your life might be spared, and how finally insinking was arrested, and you revived again.

So you enrich your own life. Then all your loved ones discover, of course, that you are filled with the higher life. And they also become filled with it along with you. And so of itself that fine state of heart is produced, which makes thanksgiving on the lips real. Impressions deepen themselves. A turning point has come into your life. And, when presently that day of thanksgiving is long again past, it will hold itself in your remembrance, it will continue to work its aftermath in you, and bring you a blessing for your own heart.

## XIX

## *"The Lord Is Good to All"*

### RESTING IN GOD'S APPOINTMENT

OUR heart is continually inclined to rebel against the
Lord our God. So really to rebel, that O, so gladly, were
it but for a single day, we would take from His hands
the reins of His supreme rule, imagining that we would
manage things far better and direct them far more
effectively than God.

This we cannot do, for His is the power, and powerlessness cleaveth unto us. But this does not take away,
that the desire for this is in us. If only we were able.
More still, that frequently umbrage passes through our
soul when we observe what God doeth, and no answer
follows upon the thousandfold questions, which continually rise in our dissatisfied and vexed heart.

This feeling is strong in us sometimes, when the
Lord offends us in our own lot in life. Then we have
our plans and prospects for the future. Sometimes even
of a very sacred and serious nature. That which is sinful
and selfish, we here pass by, because with all such
deliberations and intentions the conscience steps in between, throws us back upon ourselves, and thereby justifies God. No, really, disappointments that come when
you are in a sinful way are not so problematical to your
faith. You rather feel, that when God blows in upon
your faith, it is strengthened. But when time and again
you perceive and experience, that sinful deliberations

can work themselves out and have free play, while on the contrary, noble purposes and godly plans, which you had made, are frustrated, umbrage comes; then the soul faces a problem, which she cannot solve; and then the question so easily comes to the lips: Wherefore does the Lord let evil prosper, and wherefore does He prevent what was meant so sacredly for the honor of His Name?

THIS impression of the Divine government is frequently very grievous. In the Netherlands, Protestants and martyrs succeeded in fighting themselves free; but were not the Huguenots in France, whose martyrblood also flowed, as good as eradicated and destroyed? God the Lord lets destructive unbelief prosper in state and science. That flourishes and blooms, and scarcely knows opposition; while faith struggles, with sober means to remain standing and to keep the head erect! In the neighborhood is a saloon, which prospers and makes money like water, and close by is a Christian school, which almost succumbs under its shortages. Two men go into business, one a child of God, who is above criticism, the other a child of the world; yet the small, pious man is at the point of bankruptcy, and that competitor lays by money every year. With him every one comes to buy. And yet, it is God Who sends clients to every store; and also in commerce and trade nothing happens by chance.

You will have two children, one a son of sorrow, who disappointed the hope of your parentheart, who amounts to nothing, and sorely tries you, and by the

side of him God had given you another son, who was
the delight of your soul, because he feared God and
took his stand with holy energy. And see, God will spare
you the boy who turned away from you, and the other,
on whom hung your soul, God will take from you, and
cut him off in the early strength of his years. If now
this led to the conversion of the one who had wandered
off, you would understand it. But of this also you have
no intimation. Your sorrow remains, and the delight of
your life is taken from you.

And God doeth this.

It is not sickness, that in opposition to God's will
snatches him from you. Nothing ever happens more
surely, than the high command of the Lord's Word.
And, moreover, from Job's story you learn, that it was
God Himself, Who allowed it and Who let it, that all
these evil things should come upon His servant Job.

AND do not think, that by looking at others, you might
be comforted.

On the contrary, the more your heart goes outside
of itself, and shares life with others, and comes away
from its selfishness, the stronger from every side this
shocking problem of God's supreme rule presses upon
you.

Love increases sorrow, and the more sympathetically as child of God you enter into the life of
others, and watch the course of life around you, the more
painfully you are affected.

O, it is said so readily, that in God's providence
there is provision for every one's need.

But who then divides the goods of this earth? Does not the Lord? And is it not then painful to your human perception, to know, that there is so many a poor widow, who looks pale and thin, because with all her trying finds that she cannot earn enough for her living, while so many a rich man, squanders in extravagance great sums of money for which he never did anything, and which he simply inherited?

When there is a pestilence in the land, and you see an only son, who was the support of his poor mother, taken away, while on the street back of her house a good-for-nothing, who regards neither God nor man, is spared, is there then not something in your heart that quails.

For you would say, it lay at hand, that God employed such a pestilence to clear out from His earth a number of useless, wicked people. And see, these He lets stand, and he who was well-nigh indispensable, He takes away.

And what speaks stronger still, because it is so exclusively in God's power, He will grant unbelief all sorts of men of mighty talent and inborn genius, while Christians in all lands must struggle with mediocrity, wherein no power is.

Even in the animal world you meet with the same problems.

A hart is a noble animal, and will graze with its young, till, see, a tiger rushes from the woods, attacks and murders it amid the mortal terror of the young.

NEVER say, therefore, that God's doing justifies itself to you, as allwise and allgood.

This can say he who does *not* think deeply, he who pays *no* heed to what goes on around him, and who is already so used to the contrasts of life, that they no more affect him.

But if you have still remained young and fresh of heart, and love inspires you, and what you see happen round about you grips you, leaves you no rest and compels you to think, no, then never say, that the common course of life teaches you God's wisdom and God's love.

It is rather as though a thwarting power goes through all of life, and as though intentionally God does otherwise, than, as we honestly think, it ought to have come to pass, that in the face of what we see, *by faith alone* we should hold ourselves to God, and, *in spite* of every experience of life, should confess, that *God is good to all* (Ps. 145, 9).

And so it should certainly not be expressed. Of the why we literally know nothing. But this much is certain, that he who lives along with things at large and observes what goes on about him, can only and alone by faith hold on to the wisdom and goodness of God.

As the Psalmist puts it: "The Lord is good to all and his tender mercies are over all his works"; no, this we do not see, and this life does not show us. This can only be witnessed to by the Holy Ghost in your innermost self.

But so alone you come to the one true viewpoint, and you have a testimony concerning your God, which neither want nor death can tear out of your heart.

Then your faith in God's goodness is a conquest, which you have won with spiritual power upon the crushing contradiction of reality around you.

Then the song that God is wise and good, is no longer a child's exercise to you, which you have sung after others, but it becomes to you a psalm of life, welling up from the inward address of your soul. And then if it goes through fire, and though the waters of bitterest reality threaten to engulf you, you yet triumph, and in the face of trouble and anguish of soul, of want and suffering, of death and grave, you yet sing of the goodness of God.

And then you do not try to explain this, in which you can nohow succeed, and then you do not reason about it, as though to hang your confession of God's goodness on the cobweb of your reasoning. For then you have the high courage, to look cold-bloodedly the bitterness of your trouble in the eye, and to drink the cup of your suffering to the dregs. And then you do not hide it, that you do not understand God, that of His love you see the *contrary*, of His wisdom rather the *reverse*. But yet you hold yourself immovably fast to what your faith in you testifies, and with the Psalmist you continue to jubilate: "The Lord is good to all, *good also to me*."

## XX

## *"Thou Holdest Mine Eyes Waking"*

### SLEEPLESS NIGHTS

NOTHING is more unequally divided than the measure of care, which by God's appointment is laid upon one person and another.

Thousands upon thousands have simply no knowledge of care. They live along like children until their death. With their fixed task for the day their morning meal is ready at their waking. That work they do; that bread they eat; and when night spreads its pale shadows again, they lie down, and fall asleep.

But such is by no means the case with all. There are also those in higher and humbler circles, whose heart is burdened day by day by many and great responsibilities, by trying uncertainties of many sorts, by overmuch work, or also by distress.

What many a one puts upon himself herewith, we do not count. Imaginary trouble and anxiety does not come to us from God, but is fruit of our little faith. And he who every morning and every evening lays hold on the courage of faith to listen to Jesus' word, that we should not be careful about to-morrow, will by constant practice of faith be soon enough delivered from this unnecessary care. This imaginary care is at home with the heathen, not with God's children. And he who dares to be a disciple of Jesus, is truly liberated from this imagined care by the Son.

Suicide, which so often proved the hellish deep, into which such imaginary care at length cast its victim, is altogether spared the man of faith.

Care, which God lays upon us, never entices one to this terrible sin. Suicide is always fruit of our own, God dishonoring unbelief.

All cares, which men needlessly shoulder themselves, we here pass by in silence. We only speak of the cares which God lays upon a man; and though faith always has sufficient elasticity and more, in our struggles with those cares to keep standing, yet these cares also are sometimes dreadfully trying and heavy.

ESPECIALLY at night this tells.

Then every one is asleep. But not the man whose heart is burdened by heavy care.

He cannot sleep. His head is too full of all sorts of thoughts crossing each other, jostling each other and chasing each other. His soul is restless within him. His blood is and remains too strongly fermented. His heart throbs, that his ear catches the sound of it. And so he remains in a tension, and after brief slumberings is startled again by threatening dream-phantoms.

For him there is no refreshment, rather aggravation of unrest. For night troubles the nerves, and instead of restoring one's strength, the tormenting struggle of sleeplessness saps the same.

This can be different. With one it may simply mean *one sleepless* night, from anxiety about a grave decision, that must be made the next morning, or an important task, that must be done on that day. Then one does not sleep at all. It can also be, that constant care and over-stimulation of head and heart has turned the plague of sleeplessness into a chronic ailment, so that although at length one does sleep, yet every night upon retiring one has to struggle through again the selfsame number of trying hours. It can be, what is called acute, but it can also be chronic. Still always in its origin and nature one. Bitter fruit of an overwrought life, exceeding the measure of our powers.


IN days of sickness sleeplessness bears an entirely different character. Then it can also take place with a child, which otherwise, with his carefree life, is already asleep before he yet touches the pillow.

Then this plague does not rise from the soul, but from the body. The working is the same, but in opposite direction. The sick can even be so far gone, that he no more thinks of anything, becomes indifferent to everything, has no more care about anything, and yet is not able to sleep.

If he could sleep, he were saved.

But that saving sleep tarries; sleep-medicine may drowse him, but does not give real, healthy, natural sleep.

This comes, because the body is indisposed; because the blood burns with feverheat; because the nerves are over-excited, and because thereby the brain is continuously active, sometimes even becoming delirious.

But however different the cause may be, the effect is the same. Both he, with whom it rises from the soul, and he, with whom it rises from the body, lack that wondrous restoration of strength, that is appointed by God Almighty for the children of men in the mystery of sleep.

Sleep is an invention of God. It is His handiwork. He has thought it out and wrought it. And though no one ever succeeded yet, and no one ever will, in discovering the nature of sleep, yet, when he may wake up refreshed, every child of God thanks his Father, Who is in the heavens; for from those heavens, and by that Father, sleep in him was wrought.

---

BUT, if then God gives sleep, whence those anxious sleeplessnesses?

And to this question you find in Scripture alone again the answer, when from that deep conviction of soul Asaph tells you, that: *God held mine eyes waking* (Ps. 77, 4). Or rather, for this does not say enough, Asaph does not tell you, but God, and testifies to the Lord his Covenant-God: "Thou heldest mine eyes waking."

What wealth of piety there lies ensconsed in a single testimony of this sort.

Of God *sleep;* but of God also *sleeplessness*. No, stronger still, when Asaph lay sleepless on his bed, he knew, that it was God, Who from moment to moment held his eyes waking.

It was not, that God allowed him sleep, but that some other cause averted sleep from his eyelids.

No, no, God Himself did it.

It was God's own will, that he did not sleep.

And it was his God, Who, as with unseen fingers,

held his eyelids open, when he wanted to close them in slumber.

See, this is piety, this is faith.

When you lie down helplessly and restlessly turn on your bed, not to utter a cry now and then: "O, God, give me sleep"; but to know, to believe and to testify to God Himself, that also in that troublous sleeplessness from moment to moment you are operated upon by your God, and that nothing overtakes you, *except what He brings upon you.*

AND do you not feel, how such faith is at the same time *medicine?*

For should there not go forth from such unshaken confidence in the presence of the Lord God, also in the dark of night, also when no one knows of your suffering, a calm-producing operation upon your nervous system, as well as upon the life of your soul?

To be sure to get asleep, advice used to be given, by great power of will to concentrate one's thoughts upon a single point. Well, then, let that one point be *your God.*

So long as you remain alone with your cares and your unrest, these cares rise mountain high before you, and surround and immure you on all sides. But when your God is with you, and you are permitted to be near unto your God, then He alone becomes great, and seen in the light of His Majesty, your cares dwindle down to so much smaller dimensions.

It is a difficult task that awaits you the next day, well, that same God, Who now keeps your eyes waking, will also be with you when that daytask comes, and in the night He will have taught you, also with respect to that daytask, to trust yourself to Him alone.

Also in such troublous nights things do not go on outside of your God. Even if you slept, it would not be your sleep, that refreshes you, but your God, even as it is not your bread, but your God Who preserves you in life.

Thus when you would say: "If now God would give my sick child a night's sleep, he would recover," when your heavenly Father holds the eyes of your child waking, He still knows what He is doing.

If possible *by* sleep, but if needs be, *without* sleep, God shall hold your child in His almighty hand.

## XXI

# "The Spirit of a Man Will Sustain His Sickness"

## STRENGTH OF SPIRIT

Of Prince Bismarck it is told, that he had enough toughness of will power, to repress an attack of raging toothache. Not always; but at times when weighty problems of state were at stake, when toothache would have disabled him, he was able to perform his weighty task with seriousness and level-headedness. So did the seriousness of his sense of duty urge his spirit, and his spirit (mind) operated so powerfully upon his nerves, that thereby he brought to effect the same result which is otherwise done by chloroform or cocaine. The germ of pain was there, but the outpouring of pain in his nerves he repressed by the power of his will.

This is what the Proverb-poet expresses in a general sense as follows: *The spirit of a man will sustain his sickness* (Proverbs 18, 14, Dutch version).

As you lie on your sick-bed, you are and continue to be all your days, a *dual* being. On one hand you exist in your *soul,* and on the other you exist in your *body*.

And the struggle is to know which shall win, the power of your soul or the power of your body.

Make no haste, let not your tongue run away with you, and say not all too readily, that of course *the soul* must win, for this is by no means always true. The needs and wants of the body can be so compelling, that the

131

soul must stand aside. Exhaustion can go so far, that the spirit loses all power over the body. And when it comes to dying, the soul is not permitted even to will to retain power over the body. Then there is no help for it.

With one-sided spiritualism, with strained over-spirituality you advance here nothing. In every domain of life God's ordinances must be reverenced, with respect also to the relation between soul and body.

The struggle of your spirit in you may therefore never aim, purposely, to injure your body and withhold from it the care, which according to God's ordinance is your body's due; but must solely be applied, to prevent the influences of your body, also and particularly in sickness, from making it impossible for the spirit within you to hold its own.

Do not take that struggle too lightly.

Pain can become an overwhelming power, an emaciating weakness, especially when it violently attacks the life of the nerves, and undermines the strength of mind.

Especially in our times the condition of our nerves has become ever more precarious. They never are at rest. By the busy, restless life they are so endlessly held in tension, as to become *over*strained and then limply to give way. Sometimes so limp, that by no stimulant can they be strung again.

Our physicians call this *depression of nerves*. A pregnant word, back of which sometimes hides nameless suffering.

And this weakening of the nerves is so serious, by reason of the fact, that by those *nerves* alone the spirit in you can operate upon your body. For your nerves are, so to say, the handle by which your soul takes hold of your body. Only by your nerves can your soul reach your body.

It is these same nerves, by which your body tries to hold your soul under, and by which your soul must enter into your body.

Sparing of your nerves is therefore in very deed a demand of piety, because thereby alone you render your spirit able, to have dominion over your body.


AND yet, do not think that the real mainspring of your strength is in those nerves.

We do not discount them; indeed we count with them; for God has strung them as conducting wires between your soul and your body; but still the strength must come from your spirit.

When you have put your horse in new traces before the heavily laden wagon, these traces render excellent service; but they are of no avail, if the horse does not pull, or is not strong enough, as truck-drivers say, "to give a start." By that "giving a start" they mean that first extreme effort to set the wheels a-going. When that is done, the rest goes easier. But that first "giving a start" costs sometimes incredible exertion of strength. And thereby you recognize the merit of the horse. Is it a horse that has blood in him, you need do nothing; for then he twists and stretches and strains of himself, until the truck makes headway. But if the horse is a jade, he remains standing stock-still, and with lash and cry and push you must try to get the cart going.

And so it is with yourself.

Your nerves are the traces to the wagon; but these

traces are of no use, if the spirit in you, that must work upon the nerves, is limp and sunken-in.

Is there strength in your spirit, strength of self-perception, strength of will, strength of action, then even with weakened nerves your strong spirit will do wonders. But if your spirit is tired, languid and without elasticity, you lie on your sick-bed really as an object of contempt, as is sometimes said: "He lies there like a log."

You notice this at once with a patient; at least if you have any knowledge of the sick-bed, by having been with many sick.

Of course we do not speak here of minor ailments, of sudden affections, which occasion little pain and do not attack the system. That is really no sick-bed.

No, by sick-bed we understand that anxious condition, when there is real suffering, when the sick one becomes exhausted; when danger lurks about the bed, and it comes to the point of struggling with the spirit that is in you against your sickness.

In case of a panic, one always sees three kinds of people. People, who stand confused and petrified, and will-lessly let themselves come to grief. Other people, who at such a time with presence of mind, do wonders. And in between these two, those ordinary folks, who do no wonders, but at least let themselves be saved, and in part lend coöperation.

And these same three sorts of people you find on the sick-bed, the moment the case becomes serious.

On one hand, sufferers, who at once drop their

wings and hide their head in the feathers, and with whom literally nothing can be done. Over against this a few noble sufferers, who with wondrous presence of mind remain master of themselves, and do not suffer courage to be lost from sight. And in between these, common sick folk, who neither coöperate nor resist much.

And with an eye to these conditions, the Proverb-poet says: "The spirit of a man will sustain his sickness," and then adds so pathetically, "but a wounded spirit, who shall lift that up?"

That is to say, when on the sick-bed you find an insunken spirit in the sufferer, so little if anything can be done.

THIS, as is self-evident, is spoken altogether in terms of the natural. Spoken as it occurs with *unconverted,* and as it occurs with *converted* people.

Yet in both instances the sinful and the noble impulse are very different.

A child of God, who is right with God, knows that the sixth commandment forbids him to jeopardize his life, and thus commands him to do all in his power to sustain his life. He also knows, that, however powerless and nothing his spirit is in itself, *grace* is a mysterious power, by which faith can do all things; and also that in just such weaknesses the strength of the Lord is made perfect.

Thus he knows the commandment. He knows his own impotence. But he also knows the Fountain, from whence power flows. And now come the workings of faith, and by these workings of faith he triumphs.

Always more than conqueror through Him Who loved us.

But a converted man can also be insunken. That faith doth not operate. That the Source of strength does not glitter before the eye of the soul. And then he is very badly off, for then the sixth commandment is nothing to him, and the knowledge of his own weakness is offensive to him.

For this reason oftentimes converted people are so utterly wretched on their sick-bed, and are often put to shame by sick people of the world.

In hospitals or retreats this is not so strongly evident.

When a child of God is amid strange environment, and understands that he is watched, and realizes, that the honor of his Savior hangs by it, this high stimulus is mostly strong enough, to lift him up out of his despondency.

But when he is alone, alone with the members of his family, and thus needs not be ashamed before any, then this faithless insinking can sometimes be so shocking and offensive, that from such a sick-bed all glorifying of the Name of God is gone.


AND yet here also in most cases it exclusively depends upon what with the horse before the heavy cart is called the "getting a start."

That *first effort* to lift oneself up from his limpness and despondency, is then indeed extremely difficult and demands an incredible exertion of strength, and if the spirit in us is not of a nobler nature, that first start is not made.

But when that first start is made, and you have brought about by faith that first revival in your spirit, so that from under your sickness you come up, and now your spirit bears rule again over your sickness, then already on the evening of that day and in the morning that comes after it goes so much easier.

And then the fruit is so glorious.

For then you feel yourself ten times more free and happy. You increase the chance of recovery. You suffer less. Your inner life resumes its activity. You do good to all around you. And above all you lie no more down in your guilt, but in your way you glorify the Lord your God.

## XXII

# "*Miserable Comforters*"

## MISERABLE COMFORTERS

ELIPHAZ, Bildad and Zophar were very wise men for their times, and they could beautifully *reason* about faith; but when they were through speaking, with a single word of His lips God the Lord has vanquished them, and imposed on them as punishment, that they should ask that same Job, before whom they had reasoned so unmercifully piously, that he would pray for them.

How it must have cut, as with the blade of a sharp knife through their proud hearts, when the Lord told them: "Let Job pray for you: for him will I accept: *lest I deal with you after your folly*" (Job 42, 8).

That was it. That very wise Eliphaz, with his friend Bildad and his friend Zophar, could *reason* that one grew cold under it, but the man could not *pray*.

And Job could.

Not that Job also in his mortal anxiety allowed no sinful sounds to proceed from his lips. But with all his stammering it had been with Job a matter pertaining *to God*. Job knew he had committed no crime. He did not understand as yet the mystery of the *suffering of the righteous*.

So it seemed to him that God had *unjustly* punished him. And that Job could not brook. His God was just, of this he was sure. But why did not God make this riddle plain to him? That was what all his trouble was about. Job rebelled with all his soul, but what was at stake with him was the living God.

And this was the difference from his reasoning friends. They knew their little lesson by heart. Suffering was punishment. Job was in *bitter* affliction; therefore Job was undergoing *severe* retribution. Punishment was proportionate to one's *sin*. So Job, who was punished in an examplary manner, must also have committed *examplary* sin. And, as in anguish of soul Job was pining away, they counted this out upon their fingers before him.

O, those cold, barren reasoners!

And then they called themselves his friends!

And then it was said, that they had come *to comfort* him!

So they put Job upon the rack.


HAD Job been a narrow, cowardly soul, he would have put up with it.

But such Job was not.

Job found in his heart an invincible courage, with all the seriousness of his God-seeking heart, to challenge that barren, hollow logic-chopping. He resisted them. Writhing with pain he put them where they belonged. The web of their reasoning he tore with the lifting of his finger. And if that had to be called comforting, well, he plainly told them, *"that they were miserable comforters."* (Job 16, 2).

Furthermore, he added thereto, that if they were seated on the ashheap and he, Job, had come to comfort *them,* he would have dealt differently by them.

"I," says he, "would heap up no words against you; no, I would not shake my head regarding you; but I would strengthen you by my word."

And, by this saying, does not Job put his finger upon the wound of this cruel manner of comforting?

Heap up words, yea, this they could do, these comforters without heart. They could deceive themselves by his sorrowful appearances. They could vent their wealth of words on Job, make him hear how piously they could talk, and what beautiful phrases they could string together, and under it all in highness of heart exalt themselves above the sufferer!

And those Bildads and Zophars are still alive.

When your heart is wrenched and your soul bleeds, they come to you with a grave countenance, and make you a discourse a yard long, which is strung together of commonplaces and texts and pious phrases. And this you must hear, till your throat contracts itself, and you long for the moment, that they finally cease their talk. And the end is, that instead of having comforted you, they have made you live through yet one *painful* moment more in your sorrow and grief.

Oн, they who so comfort have never been at school with the Divine Comforter.

They know not the *Christus Consolator*. They understand not that touching weeping of Jesus over Jerusalem. Cursorily they read, without thought, what is written, that Jesus "was moved with inward compassion," and "became greatly moved in spirit." And above all they know not the inner work of the Holy Ghost, that Comforter of the troubled heart. What "divine pity" is, is still a mystery to them.

They speak too much about the Cross, and have sat too little in reverent worship at the foot of that Cross. That God's Son, Who is Himself God, to comfort us, became flesh, to suffer *with* us and to suffer *for* us, by them has never been understood.

And when to a poor soul, that is plunged in mourning and anguish, two comforters enter in, of which one has a tear in the eye, and quietly presses the hand, and keeps silent; and the other holds a beautiful discourse; then the people of superficialities think in themselves: Oh, the first, he was a great comforter, he never said a word; but the last, he did it beautifully!

But that poor soul in her anguish of heart thought *differently*. That tear in the eye was sweet unto her. With that gentle pressure of hand something of blessed comfort thrilled in the heart. And when that reasoning person began, ice formed around the heart, and there was relief, when he ended.

No, comforting lies not *in words*.

Words too can comfort. But one must go differently about it. First the eye must have spoken, and the expression of the face and the warm hand-clasp. And when thus the soul disclosed herself and drew breath again, then first a gentle, whispering word; and when thus the sorrowing soul herself begins to speak, then, yea, further conversation can follow; not with a little lesson learned by rote; not with reasoning ready-made for all who are in sorrow; but with *language of the heart*.

ALL the difference is, whether you *love,* or whether you come to pay your *compliments.* When the sorrow and grief of such a troubled soul leaves you *cold,* you can minister no comfort; you have no power to do it. For to comfort is to lighten sorrow. And you can lighten no sorrow, when you take no part of that sorrow upon yourself.

To comfort is no hushing with soft talk, but suffering oneself with the sufferer; sharing distress with him who is distressed. With the troubled of soul feeling pain in your own heart.

There is no comforting, where there is no fellowship of heart with heart. Then you whitewash and plaster and paint with pious sounds, but they do not enter in. The heart must open, that comfort may be carried into it, and by your frozen words you close it.

*Love* is the soul of all real comforting. Forgetting yourself. Thinking of the aggrieved one alone. Entering into the life of anguish. *Living along* with it. If we may say so, putting up connecting lines, along which the sorrow and the anguish from that troubled soul pass over *into* your soul, and along which in turn from your heart comfort passes over into the heart of the one so bitterly afflicted.

Not as though there is power in much weeping. O, even as there are two kinds of words, so there are two kinds of tears. There are tears that are shed from heartfelt compassion, and these are *few.* But there are also tears which rise from the *nerves,* and these are passionate. The latter affect also the nerves of the afflicted; but the former, deep welled-up tears reflect in their sheen something heavenly for his *heart.*

Thus not much commotion. Not much clamor. Sor-

row is suffered in silence. There is something sacred
about it.

Or to say it otherwise. He who comes to bring comfort, must first have prayed for grace to be able to
minister comfort. He who comes *alone*, cannot do it.
Only he who *with his God* enters the tent of affliction,
understands of this wondrous comforting the mystery.
Heartfelt compassion is never from us. It must always
be quickened in our soul by the Lord our God.

But then, also, when this heartfelt pity, when something of this divine compassion has wakened in you,
never ask beforehand what you shall say.

Then go in this your strength, and in that hour
the Holy Ghost will give you what to say.

And if possible, when you are alone with the bitterly afflicted one, and in the end there has been a full
disclosure of heart to heart, kneel down with the troubled of heart before your and his God.

Only as you pray together to the God of all comfort, does the full, rich comforting drop as balsam into
the wound, that bleeds.

## XXIII

# *"A Sharp Thorn in the Flesh"*

### SATAN IN OUR SUFFERING

In II Cor. 12, 7, Paul writes: "And lest I should be exalted above measure through the abundance of the revelations, there was given me a sharp thorn in the flesh, the messenger of Satan to buffet me, lest I should be exalted above measure."

What particular suffering St. Paul underwent, is not told us, and every surmise regarding it is merely a fruitless effort, to satisfy the stimulus of curiosity.

You do well, therefore, *not* to indulge this stimulus.

It brings you no further, and prevents you from gathering the fruit, that in this brief report from Paul's life Scripture offers you.

Suffice it, that Paul suffered.

While hundreds and thousands of gay spirits, from whose lives, as we would say, nothing was lost, at Corinth as well as at Athens, revelled in the freshness of perfect strength, the great apostle of the Lord, who was called to lead the most wearing of lives, and to travel around half the then known world, had to carry the load of anxious and bitter suffering.

Not a suffering from youth up, but an impairment of physical strength, that overtook him, just when the Lord had brought him to the height of his apostolic ministry and spiritual ecstasy had taken most powerful hold of him.

Then it was that his health broke down; and he was overtaken by virulent and bitter suffering, which he could not describe better, than by saying, that it seemed to him, as though a demon assaulted him and beat him with fists.

And then Paul had prayed indeed that that suffering might be taken away from him; but the Lord had *not* taken it away.

He would indeed receive abundant grace to bear it patiently; but that grace had to be sufficient for him.

Just to reveal the power of that grace, Paul had to be afflicted with that suffering.

For himself, that with his soul he might enter the more deeply into the sweetness of that grace.

For the churches of his time, that they might the more highly admire the divine origin of so powerful an apostolate in an apostle physically broken down such as he.

And no less for believers of all ages, that when God afflicts them in the body, they too might understand the purpose of their suffering, and in case their prayers are not heard might *not* fall away from their faith.

FOR in such painful and oppressive physical suffering S. Paul does not stand alone.

Such suffering has age upon age troubled many believers. And to this day in every city and in every village you find those, who reading this troubled word of Paul, are at once reminded of a thorn in their own flesh, and from whose lips falls the complaint: "So it also took hold of me."

Such suffering takes on all sorts of forms.

At one time it is deafness or weakness of vision. At another weakness of lungs and difficulty in breathing. Then again painful sickness, facial neuralgia, or stiffness of joints. There are also results of a fall, of a delicate operation, or the after-effects of an illness. Altogether changing forms, wherein this one great evil appears, by which our health is impaired; by which we are hindered in our elastic utterance of life; and whereby every time again courage is extinguished in our spirit.

And, especially when it is a lingering illness, it is so hard to bear, because then in most instances sympathy on the part of those around us grows languid, and finally dies down altogether.

O, when suddenly you are stricken down by an acute illness, or some accident overtakes you, then the compassion of human sympathy flows toward you from every side; then every one does his best to help you; and the comfort of love is so great and so sweet.

But when this goes on for days and weeks, and the suffering does not abate, then our environment *adapts* itself to our pitiable condition. One becomes so *accustomed* to the sight of our suffering. What good is it to say much more about it? Things are as they are. Such is our lot. And in the end one knows no better, than that such and not otherwise is our permanent state.

But the sufferer himself does *not* become accustomed to it. To him every morning the affliction is new, and every evening he pours out again his complaint before his God.

Ineradicably the sense, that we were not created to suffer, continues to struggle against the pain, that restlessly accompanies him upon his pathway through life.

And when daily he sees so many around him, who strong and happy and in full enjoyment of health live the rich life of earth, who then averts the sad complaint from his lips: "O, My God, why am not I as they"?

So Satan mingles himself in all such unbearable suffering.

He, the evil demon, who is always bent upon disturbing our peace, spurs us on, to murmur against that thorn in the flesh.

First he whispers in our ear, that we should pray God, to deliver us from it. "If then you are a child of God, where is your heavenly Father, to help you?"

And then one prays.

He prays ever more ardently: "O, God, Thou canst deliver me. Thou hast delivered so many. Deliver also me."

But no answer comes.

The suffering keeps on.

Sometimes it even increases, rather than grows less.

And then Satan whispers a new temptation in the soul, and asks: "Where is now your God?"

A mocking of your faith. A holding up of your prayer to ridicule. A flouting of your God, Whom you loved.

And then additionally, pain becomes the more severe and makes the spirit in us the more uneasy, so that our soul loses her equipoise altogether, and then, without any one having any intimation of it, such a temptation can become so demoniac, so satanic, that there have been sufferers, who actually for months and years fell away from their faith; cursed God; and rebelliously and angrily shut themselves up in the bitterness of their own heart.

But it can also be *otherwise;* and frequently it is different.

When the soul may come to realize, that God the Lord can also order such suffering of His child, the more richly and the more fully to reveal in him the majesty of His grace.

Then also at first prayer is made for deliverance, and rarely is that prayer silenced altogether.

But yet, the soul at length becomes convinced, that in such suffering God intends something different with us.

That such suffering does not come upon us by chance, but comes to us from Him, and that He chose us to bear this suffering, that in this our suffering it might become evident, even with suffering most prolonged and most bitter, what sacred medicine of soul grace is.

And if the eye might but open to this, O, then each day brings experience of new grace; till finally the spirit made willing in us begins to coöperate with grace, to triumph over this suffering and to show Satan and the world, that the happiness God's child enjoys, is too rich and too abounding, to be shadowed even by severest suffering.

And so at times sufferers have been seen, who were so gloriously disciplined *by* grace and in grace, that at the last it seemed, as though they had become insensible to their trouble, yea, that they took pleasure in it, with a heavenly smile upon their face to mock their suffering.

YET Christian love suffers loss, when he who lives in the environment of such a sufferer, takes advantage of that exalted state of grace, and, because of the jubilation on the part of the sufferer in the midst of his distress, forsakes the duty of compassion.

He who loves of himself suffers sympathetically along with the sufferer, and he who can witness suffering, without feeling this sympathy in his heart, has extinguished love in himself.

And that must not be in a family, where the Name of Jesus is invoked, because it antagonizes the Cross.

He has borne our sicknesses, and the Cross of Golgotha ever remains the holy symbol, that continuously calls upon us to weep with those who weep, and by taking a part of their suffering upon ourselves, to lighten the cross they carry.

This must be done *for their sakes*, because as priests and priestesses of God we have to minister unto them something of the love of God.

This must be done *for our* own *sakes*, because only the hardened egoist eats up his own happiness, and is not willing that trouble of others shall spoil it.

And above all this must be done *for God's sake*.

For sovereign-like He portions out sorrow and joy in most unequal measures, that by that very inequality, he who suffers, should find a hand of love to grasp; and he whose cup thus far has been nothing but joy, should extend the hand of seeking, serving, and comforting to the sufferer.

## XXIV

## *"Looking Unto the Chief Leader"*

### SUFFERING AND THE MAN OF SORROWS

OUR fathers have banished the crucifix also from the
sick-room and from the deathbed; and this notwithstand-
ing the fact that already for so long centuries it had
been in use among all Christians.

They did this, not as though by itself there was
something wrong or sinful in the possession of a small
cross; nor as though they denied, that the sight of such
a cross could direct the otherwise distracted thoughts
again to "Christ and him crucified"; but because it was
evident, that such crucifixes could lead to unspiritual
abuse.

Neither in the Gospels, nor in the other Scriptures
of the New Testament did they read anything, that sug-
gested orders to make use of such crucifixes; on the contrary, every time again souls were directed to look "upward, where Christ is," "Whom we no longer know after
the flesh."

And when it was observed, how the crucifix was put
up in all sorts of places; not least in inns and bar-rooms,
where blasphemies, drunken bouts and revelries were
the order of the day, it was perceived but all too painfully, how the crucifix had become a sort of magical
expedient, that had been loosened from its spiritual
background.

Sense and tendency to hold high the spiritual character of our Christian religion, has then led among us to the entire dismissal of the crucifix.

Also our sick and dying should not look with sensual eye to a cross of ebony, but fix the spiritual eye upon the Christ in the heavenly sanctuary; and the means every time again to lead up to that Christ in the heavens, was not the crucifix, but the Word.

ONLY let us herewith be on our guard against one very serious danger, not arrogantly to look down upon Roman Catholics because of their crucifix, and meanwhile, do, not only without crucifix, but also without Savior.

And yet, alas, to this it has come in many of our families that call themselves Protestant, that one objects to a crucifix, but feels no compunction whatsoever, when there is a long sick-bed and sometimes even a deathbed at which Christ Himself in the love of His Mediatorship is not known.

So first the crucifix is removed, and afterward the soul estranged from Christ, and it is no more understood, that many a lover of a crucifix will go into the Kingdom of heaven before you, who even on your sick-bed could deny the Savior.

Our fathers have never opposed Romish practices merely to help these practices out of the world. Their purpose always was in the place of the lower and questionable use that had crept in, to put something of higher spirituality. And you also, you are not worthy to call yourselves sons of the church of the martyrs, when you are strong in opposing Romish misuse, but ignore that revelation of higher, richer, fuller spiritual life, in which glistens the honor of Christ.

No crucifix, but then also Christ Himself at your sick-bed. And when you die not clasping with your hands a cross of ebony, but clasping Christ with all the love of your soul.

REGARDING all suffering, including therefore also suffering on sick-bed and dyingbed, the holy apostle exhorts you in so touching a manner: *"Let* us run with patience the race that is set before *us, looking unto the chief Leader and Finisher of the faith,* JESUS CHRIST!" (Hebr. 12, 2, Dutch version).

Had not that Christ Himself testified through Isaiah (53) that He would take *our sicknesses upon Himself,* and that He *would carry our sorrows?*

And does there not unravel itself from the combination of these divine utterances an holy mystery of comfort, in which he who is sick or is at the point of death can so blessedly refresh himself?

For what is your most serious illness else than one single drop from that cup of God's wrath, which your Savior has emptied to the dregs, emptied also for you?

The words of eternal retribution and hellish doom are so readily spoken, but have you ever thought painstakingly, what unexpressed weight of suffering and of distress of soul would come upon you, if for but one moment God's holy anger would spend its full strength upon the sinful in your heart and against the guilt of your past?

And yet, that deep suffering and that soul-cutting

anguish your Jesus has borne for you, and whatever as after-effect operates in your illness and in your dying, is nothing save the little crumbs of anguish, which you gather up after Him.

And does it not already comfort and cast upon your suffering an altogether other light, when also in your suffering you see that chief Leader go out before you, to carry for you and in your place the real sorrow which would consume you, and leave nothing for you to do save to come after Him, not with the heavy cross that would crush you, but with the, O, comparatively so little cross, that *gladly following* you carry after him?

ALSO when Jesus performed His miracles and healed the sick at Capernaum, the Evangelist tells us, that again in another way that same prophecy of Isaiah regarding the bearing of our sicknesses was fulfilled.

And though Jesus is no longer on earth now to heal our sick, this still addresses our sick so comfortingly, provided love for Jesus is warm in them.

That He then healed the sick, was not the indifferent act of a magician, who exhibits his mysterious art. With Jesus there spoke in that healing of the sick divine and yet again also human compassion.

Jesus saw the insunkenness, saw the exhaustion, saw the pains and the sorrows of the sick, which were brought to Him, and these filled Him with a compassion, the like of which has never thrilled our heart.

His accompanying and therefore sympathizing love went so deep. Far deeper even than the sick themselves,

Jesus felt for them and with them all the sorrow and misery, in which they lay submerged.

So by the wondrous power of His compassion of soul He took their suffering upon Himself, and so it was, *bearing their sickness*, that He healed their sickness.

And this same Savior is now also exalted, and is alive in the sanctuary above, and by His majesty, grace and Spirit He can be present in every sick-room, at every deathbed.

And is there then no mysticism of comfort in it, when God's child may perceive, feel, experience: No one who better understands my suffering than Jesus fathoms it; that Jesus Who is still alive, Who lives to pray also for me; and Who, with every new storm of trouble and distress that breaks loose upon me, sends that hidden grace, that also from this storm delivers me?

AND yet, for him who is sick and suffering and is menaced by death, there is in that looking unto the chief Leader still something more, still something different toward which faith directs itself.

For on the way of sorrow and suffering that chief Leader has Himself gone before us.

He, the Blessed of the Father, came into this world to the music of angel songs; but how soon was that rejoicing of the heavenly hosts silenced, to give place to the cries of hatred and vengeance, presently answered by the tears and strong cryings, wherewith your Savior, though He was the Son, has cried before his God.

In this world without God it could not become for

God's Son anything else than a whole life of suffering.

Suffering after the soul, and suffering after the body, as our Catechism puts it, "all the time of His life"; and therefore "Man of sorrows" is a name expressive of so inexpressibly much.

And when you may gaze upon that suffering Messiah, and direct your eye to that cross of Christ, and compare with it your own suffering, does not then your own suffering shrink in its dimensions?

When you see Him bear that suffering, carry that cross, and die on that cross, though He was the Holy One, solely to save sinners; and you turn back again into your own sinful heart, and go back to your own guilty past, and you compare what is laid upon you with what He carried, are you not then almost ashamed, that so little came upon you?

And where as child of God, as one redeemed by your Savior, you have to pass through that same world, and must go out from that same world, in which your Jesus has carried so heavy a burden, does it not seem natural to you, that suffering has also made its approach to you, yea, is it not then as though that suffering brings you closer to your Jesus, makes you more of a sharer of the same lot with Him, and becomes to you a mark of holy fellowship with the Man of Sorrows?

O, there is nothing deeper than the mystery of Gethsemane and the mystery of Golgotha, and no song can ever voice and no human language express, what in hours of bitter anguish and hard death-struggle by faith God's dear children have tasted and enjoyed of strength and comfort and refreshment of soul from that cross.

And that same cross still works its wonders, when

in us there may but operate that pondering love, that mysticism of faith, which confirms also upon our sickbed and in our dying the "no more I live, but Jesus liveth in me."

## XXV

## *"Who Giveth Psalms in the Night"*

### WATCHING

Do you know the tension, but also the sweet, of watching in the nightly hour by the bedside of your sick? To watch, not for money, but from love. As a mother watches by the little cradle, when the breathing of her darling is more than normally quick, and the doctor said there was cause for anxiety, and the motherheart fears the worst.

Such watching is always a sacrifice, especially in days when anxious care fills the heart. Then the nerves have to bear so much. Everything always storms again upon those strained and overstrained nerves, that have no time to recuperate themselves. And then for this over-strained life of the nerves sleep is really the only medicine; that wondrous sleep, when God takes you into His inner chamber and into His darkness, and takes weariness away from you and fills you with fresh vigor of life.

And in such days, to refuse that only medicine, that is able to restore to you your feeling of rest, and to say: "Let the others take rest, *I will watch*," in all seriousness, there belongs to this an energy of love and will power and quiet devotion, which no less than alms and prayer of faith has its reward with God.

Such watching is something altogether different from that of the strange nurse, who sleeps by day, and comes for the night, and at the bedside reads her book.

Not that there is not something noble in this, and that this love also should not be appreciated; but yet watching, taken in its deepest sense, is when one is no stranger, but member of the family; when all day long the tension of the sick-bed has been endured; and now, at the approach of night, and while the others go to sleep, bears all the care not only, but all the uneasiness of the sick upon the heart.

Therefore, in such watching there is something of a priestly act. Oneself to keep awake that the sick might sleep.

That priestly wakefulness which also Christ in Gethsemane sought with His three most faithful disciples, but without finding it, when He said: "Could ye not watch with me one hour?"

THIS watching differs much, according to the nature of the illness.

Watching may be necessary with a typhoid patient, who is delirious, and who observes nothing of the offering of love that is brought him. Which watching is therefore so doubly wearing, because as a rule such a patient breaks the stillness of the sick-room all night long with wild outcries; care for the sick one is restlessly continued; and all fear of being oneself infected must be overcome by the power of love.

Different again is the watching, when on the sick-bed much is suffered in unbearable pain or frequently recurring attacks of shortness of breath. Then one would do everything to hush the pain, but stands by impotent to bring relief.

O, there is in suffering such endless variegation. One sick-bed differs so greatly from the other. Also spiritually, whether you watch with one who knows the Fountain of Life, and also on the sick-bed tastes something of the hidden Manna, or whether your patient is still engaged with his own trouble alone, and in the deepest depth of his heart still rebels against his God and his Savior.

Some sick people are so dear, with whom to watch even in part is a delight, so grateful are they for all you do; so satisfied with everything no matter with what result, so almost overcome with the exhibition of your love. But there are also others who exhaust almost all your patience; who take all your love for something that speaks of itself; who leave you no moment's rest, and want now this, now that, till at length you can do no more.

And therefore you cannot estimate all watching as of one kind, and there are degrees of love and devotion so different, that watching with one demands far more from you than with the other.

But under all these forms, in all watching, the one heavenly thought continues to sustain you: "For my sick one it is necessary, for my sick one it is good."

Now such watching is most beautiful, when it may go on quietly, and when a splendid narcotic operates wholesomely upon the patient, and he may slumber if not all night, but yet off and on for one or two hours at a time.

In many cases sickness gives a feeling of uneasiness, and when the evening shadows fall, the nerves of the sufferer become generally yet more restless. Then being alone affects him so painfully, and every time he looks around, to see whether there is any one with him.

And, O, then the reward is so sweet, which God gives you at the hand of your patient, when you see that your presence affords him quiet, and so the contented knowledge that you sit there by the bedside, at length pacifies the unrest in his heart and in his nerves, and from his breathing you observe, that he slumbers.

This then can become so delightful, that in the end you forget the weariness of watching, and you have more joy in the fact that your sick one is asleep, than sleep of your own would bring you.

And when the watcher for a time hears nothing more, and softly on tiptoe approaches the bed, to see how things are, and finds the poor sufferer, with an expression of relaxation on the face, sunken away in quiet sleep, O, then the heart thrills with delight, and then not infrequently he who kept awake gives thanks for him who sleeps.


SOMETIMES even such watching, already that very night, has still greater reward.

Elihu spake to Job of a God Who giveth psalms in the night (Job 35, 10), and he who in watching was permitted to hold converse with God, has well understood this word of Elihu.

That quiet watching, when everything in the house is at rest, and the patient himself at length went to sleep, brings, with the dusk of the turned-down light, frequently such sacred emotions to the soul.

One is then so *altogether* alone, and yet *not* lonely, for especially in such quiet nights comes One, Whom no one sees, to watch with us, and to watch over our soul.

The seriousness of life is then all around us. That sick-bed makes all sorts of anxious questions to rise in the heart. Will it be unto death, or will there still be a return to life? All the memories of the anxious activities of the day pass through the mind. What shall it be again to-morrow? God alone knows. From anxiety you come, and when the morning breaks, you face new anxiety and new care.

So you forget the world; you scarcely think of yourself; the problems of death and eternity take you by storm; and now, in the stillness of night, in that semi-darkness, it seems to God's child, that his God comes nearer to him, that his faithful Shepherd comes to look after him, and that his Father in heaven, full of divine compassion comes to sustain him, to renew his strength, and in spite of all that weighs upon his heart to comfort him.

AND in *that* sense watching is sometimes, O, so sweetly enjoyed among us.

Not when one reads a novel to keep awake. For all such reading diverts you from your patient, brings you into another world, and leads your thoughts out to strange fictions.

No, real watching is when in soul and thoughts one keeps busy with the sick; keeps busy with his distresses; and when in conflict of soul, the heart is turned unto prayer, and the Holy Ghost prays for and with you with groanings that cannot be uttered.

That then relaxes your soul, not by diverting her, but by deepening your life in your God, by directing your deliberations toward Him, and now to find, O, such fullness of peace in His mysterious doings, in His wondrous dealings with your poor sick.

And then of itself comes the psalm. Not to be sung aloud, as though your patient was not to be spared.

No, but the silent psalm, to the accompaniment of the organ of your heart, and your soul jubilates, though no sound passes your lips.

Inner motions in the depth of your heart, expressing themselves in that unspoken language, which even your patient does not hear, but which your Comforter within you overhears.

Psalms welling up in you, because in the stillness of the night God has come to you with His holy breath, and has restored harmony, equipoise in the turmoil of your heart.

A psalm, because peace is returned within. A psalm, because in such perfect confidence you give over your sick one to your God. A psalm, because already in your own soul you feel, that this sickness also will eventuate in the glorifying of God's Name.

In daytime it cannot be so. Then there is too much going on. Then there is too much that requires attention. Then everything distracts.

But by night this becomes different. Then you do not look for the doctor. Then no one knocks at the door. Then you need not to be ready for him who comes to visit your patient.

And therefore in those long nights of watching, with serious illness, there is so glorious a strengthening of soul. Soul's strengthening going out in psalms, which your God gives you.

## XXVI

## *"Sick, and Ye Visited Me"*

### NURSING OUR SICK

To take care of one who is really sick is always a *sacred* duty.

*Sacred,* because your God appoints it so, that not you, but your sick one lies upon the sick-bed; and that your sick one, on the other hand, lies helpless and cannot manage himself without your help. So the Lord casts down one upon the sick-bed and leaves the other in health, that both together might be an exhibition of His divine ordinance.

But this caring for our sick is also sacred *for Christ's sake.*

Our human nature is no more left to itself. Christ has assumed it. Everything human stands thereby related to His Mediator-heart. And as once upon the cross He took our sicknesses upon Himself, so this day He sees in every sick person a silhouette of His own suffering. And so He set it as a rule: "Inasmuch as ye have done it unto one of the least of these my brethren, ye have done it unto Me. In them I was sick, and when you then surrounded them with your love, that love applied unto Me" (S. Matt. 25, 40).

What glow of love by this single word Jesus has made to burst into flame, cannot be told in words. That one word has done wonders. And when through all these twenty centuries, among all sorts of people and nations, there have ever been thousands upon thousands, who laid down sick and helpless, and in their helplessness underwent tender nursing, nursing in which spake the language of the heart, they owed it all to this one word of Jesus.

That one saying: "Inasmuch as ye have done this unto one of the least of these my brethren, ye have done it unto Me," has operated like an electric spark, leaping from heart to heart.

The eye, more yet, the compassionate heart, has opened to what for the amelioration of suffering human love could provide. By tender nursing to take part of the suffering from the sick upon oneself, has become a sacred art, wherein one vies with the other.

Especially woman's heart has herewith revealed its inventiveness and its inexhaustible elasticity.

And this whole movement, which in hospitals, in Sisters of Charity, in the Red Cross, in the White Cross, and what not else, exhibits its glittering afterglow, from what else has it borrowed its motive, and in what else has it found its never dulling stimulus, except in that one, deeply mystical word of Jesus: "I was sick, and ye visited Me."

AND yet, though the broad stream of compassion with our sick, which since that royal word has gone out into the world, is one in origin, there is in that care for our sick a twofold direction, which must carefully be distinguished.

One is domestic; the other more public.

So there may be two young women, one of whom by day and by night, unbeknown to the world, and herself not fathoming the depth of her devotion, cares for an aged, sick grandmother or an incurable sick little brother; while the other in uniform walks the street, attends meetings, goes from house to house, and is known to the public as a neighborhood or hospital nurse.

The first direction is more along the Protestant line; the other, as soon as it becomes predominant, inclines more to the Romish type.

This does not mean, to dissuade the sisters among us who do nursing outside from their calling, for very surely public nurses also are highly necessary. Neither that we deem, that in Romish families there is not also sometimes very tender care bestowed upon the sick; we would not even rob the Jew of this honor.

We only mean, that our Protestants incline more readily, to make also this glorious side of the Christian religion to glisten more brightly in the ordinary domestic circle, while Rome inclines more to set a domain apart also for this utterance of life.

In all Romish countries hospitals and asylums are therefore also far more extensive than with us. The several orders of Sisters of Mercy, of every name and title, are altogether of Romish origin. And it is difficult to deny, that the meritoriousness of care for the sick among them was always a strong stimulus.


So it was not among us, at least not in the palmy days of the Church of the Reformation, and except in sporadic cases the need of outside nursing was not felt.

Love among the members of the family mutually

was then at a far higher level, and especially the mother held very high rank.

For however plain the quiet housemother seemed in her doings and non-doings, and however little she might be developed in literary respect, she stood high in the knowledge of what belonged to life "within doors." To make the bed soft; to arrange pillows in such a way as to afford most comfort; to provide covering that was warm and yet not too heavy; to temper the light in the sick-room; to care for pure, fresh air; tenderly to prepare suitable food and drink for the invalid's tray; and with it all to be gently voiced, tender and sympathetic in her manner; O, all this applied as a sort of family tradition to the sick-bed, which was handed on among our housemothers from generation to generation.

There was little going out; more time was spent in the inner room, than in sitting at the window; and so the eye and the mind and the question of the heart turned inward; to the inside of domestic life; and led it up in this respect to such high perfectness; a degree of perfection the more glorious, because there was no temptation of seeking self in it.

Such a quiet housemother scarcely remembered, that Jesus had said: "Inasmuch as ye did this to the least of these my brethren, ye did it unto Me."

She did it without much thought about it.

From inward urge of commiseration and sense of duty.

And therefore she could belong to the many, whom Jesus refers to as saying: "When saw we Thee sick, and came unto Thee?"

For they are indeed the very noblest of our race, who lead a beautiful life of love, without themselves knowing how high they stand, and by this very *not* knowing are spared much spiritual sin.

YET let no one be unreasonable.

For they who do outside nursing, have also in turn something, in which they can stand spiritually higher.

For mother at home never nurses any one except her own husband, or the child that she has carried under her heart, or a father who lives with her. So here love germinates, which must do wonders at the sick-bed, from the blood relationship, from the love that was already present in the heart. Natural love and love for Christ's sake here flow in one.

But such is *not* the case with those who nurse outside.

There we face a sick person who is strange to us; who neither as blood relative nor as friend can lay a claim to our heart; and whom now we are to care for in his sickness; because we have devoted ourselves to this service of love, joined ourselves to a house of mercy, and by those who direct this house, have been sent to this sick person, whether in hospital or in a private house.

That one seeks out such a needy patient, and of one's own volition cares for him, also occurs, but yet most seldom. Almost always one is sent to this or that sick one.

It is not a matter here of money; for when payment is made, that money goes into the treasury of the house.

The nurse herself has but a small part of it and

spends her life in watching, in assisting and in caring for the sick.

And now it speaks for itself, that an entirely other stimulus must operate in the heart, with such an one who is altogether a stranger, often sick with a repulsive disease, sometimes in a hovel, in which every convenience is wanting, in the midst of poverty, for which there is no help, and with almost no appliances at hand, to quiet pain and ameliorate distress.

With all this a far greater straining of love is required, therefore, than with the housemother in her own family.

If only we may have an eye for it, that that very higher demand brings also a spiritual danger of its own.

Every one knows it of us; we know it so well of ourselves; in all this work of love there is so much that shows on the outside; and from this springs for our guileful heart so often a false stimulus.

OF course the glorious promise of Jesus applies only to that care for the sick, which in its impulse and incentive remained *pure*.

To be able to plead this glorious promise, you must nurse your sick from love; from nothing but love; from that love which suffers along with the patient; and from compassion tries to take that suffering upon yourself and to ameliorate it.

Every secondary aim does injury to the sacred character of this compassion among people.

There must be no ambition to be over-active, no seeking of self-honor, no imagination of one's own excellency, else it all remains the *tinkling* cymbal of I Corinthians 13.

And therefore let one be on guard.

To go out nursing among strangers is in many cases necessary, and may God strengthen such as devote themselves to this ministry of mercy.

But let no one be taken to the hospital who can be cared for at home.

And then, let every young woman examine herself, whether she would be equally ready, equally patient and equally regular in nursing the sick in her own home as she is willing to do this among strangers.

## XXVII

## *"Thou Changest All His Bed in His Sickness"*

### IN HIS SICKNESS THOU CHANGEST HIS BED

OUR *sick!* O, who spells for us the overrunning measure of secretly suffered anguish and hidden pain, that lies back of that "our sick"! Little is known of it, but behind curtains many an anxious scene is enacted. In the sick-room what illusions are cut off, what friendly little lights are extinguished, what flowers broken at the stem. And then at times, moreover, those physical *pains*. Pain is so deeply grievous. And then those *long*-continued pains. That there is no end to them. And that it cuts so deep and gnaws as it were at our bones. A veil hangs before it. People at large have little knowledge of it. But yet "our sick," it is a separate world, and safely add, a dreadful world, at least so long as one must suffer in it *without his God.*

Do you think much about these "sick"? Do they live in your prayer? Are they, not formally, but with pity and compassion, remembered in the prayers of the Church on the Lord's days?

They are *"our* sick," and you feel what that implies. "Our" sick, who belong to *us*, who from *our* circles, from *our* church, from *our* living-rooms, went to the *sick-room*; of our flesh and our blood.

"Our sick," who lie there, to say something to us, to arrest us in our playfulness, to tell us: "Presently it

172

comes to you." *Our* sick, who became sick that we
should practice our love on them, that *our* faith should
become manifest to them, that comfort should come at
*our* lips. *Our* sick, who lie down in white robes as priests
and priestesses, softly to whisper to us: *"Only through
and because of sin;* thus also because of and for you!"
Yea, why hold it back in the pen, in our depraved and
corrupting life "our sick" are a salt that averts corruption. If those sicknesses had not come, how many souls
would never have found their God, how much devotion
and self-denial would never have unfolded, how much
more unbridled the merry-making of the world would
gallop along its undulating path? Sicknesses, they are an
arresting grace for all our circle of life. And that is the
glory of our sick that lie down. They think they are
doing nothing, and see, they bless us. They deem that
all their suffering is for nought, and yet their sorrows
are a cement for God's house.

Wonderful, is it not? Because otherwise it would go
beyond all limits in wantonness and playfulness; God
sends an angel who smites, and from the viol of this
angel there falls here and there a drop of wrath upon a
dear ruddy child, which pales and emaciates, and yonder
falls a drop upon a consecrated child of God, who was
zealously at work for the Lord of hosts and is now suddenly arrested in his course.

Why, you would say in your fancy, why, when
there must be sick, does not God's ban strike the godless
or the aged, who must pass on anyway?

And, of course, so long as "being sick" is to you
a purposeless waste of time, it cannot be understood.
But when you realize that "being sick" is a discipline
of strength in the Kingdom, that by that "being sick"

God binds the devil in society and makes tenderest devotion to unfold, O, then it becomes altogether different. Then you understand that a sick person sometimes is far more useful and accomplishes far more for the Lord than a man, who walks about in his strength. And then it will also dawn upon you, why time and again God brings sickness upon so many of His dearest children. For they are the persons through whose sickness He can accomplish most. God's dear children always have other children of God, who love them tenderly. So devotion comes into play most beautifully. God's dear children are Satan's most favorite targets. So they need a heavier weight on the clock of their soul than other people. And also, from their dying bed more can go out from God's dear children than from the children of the world.

Rivet and Witsius were both highly learned professors. And yet it is the question whether by the few days of their sick-bed they did not make contribution of more intrinsic merit to the building up of the Kingdom of God than by their learned treatises. We cannot make true reckonings of this, but the spiritual power of a God-glorifying sick-bed reaches so endlessly far. It is a spark that ignites and from which ignition new sparks are again ignited; from generation to generation. So sinks the grain of wheat away into the ground, but always new grains ripen on the top of the stalks!

And whether then God does no wrong?

No injustice by imposing this distress upon His dearest children?

Think of Golgotha! "He was wounded for our transgressions! Through His stripes our healing." And at once you would take back your question, would you not?

But, no, don't do that. Have something of Job's courage and with him say to your Comforter: "God's cause is in no need of palliation! I will speak to the Almighty, and I will reason with God" (Job 13, 3).

FOR truly there is a solution.

God the Lord does no wrong when He lays affliction upon His dearest children, "for," says the Spirit by David (Ps. 41, 3): "Thou changest all their bed in sickness!" (See Rev. Ver. marg.)

A God, Who has such hidden power, may freely risk His dearest children to it.

For "changing all their bed" what is this mystery?

Is it not Mara?

Israel that, weary of the pilgrim-journey, in the wilderness comes to a well, but cannot drink the waters; for see, those waters were bitter. And then Israel's shepherd called upon the Lord, and the Lord showed him something. He cast it into the well. And see, the bitter water became sweet. And then Israel continued their pilgrim-journey, and found twelve fountains of water and seventy palm trees, and they encamped around those waters.

For this, truly this, is the sacred mystery of God's dearest children, when they go through the wilderness of sicknesses: *God changes everything for them.*

Sometimes not. Then He goes away and leaves them alone. Be it because they had not loved Him, be it because their love had to be put to the proof! And then it is dreadful. Then roarings ascend from the abysses of their soul within them. Then rebellion settles down upon them as a dark cloud, pierced only now and then by a lightning-flash of faith.

But that does not last. Soon or late the Lord comes back, and then a miracle takes place. For then everything remains as it was; perhaps the sickness becomes even worse; and yet nothing in it is as it was before. "In sickness God has changed all his bed!"

It remains bitter and yet it has become sweet.

Because the Lord came and took hold of the soul and inbreathed power from within and comforted with His tenderest comfortings.

And then a way of faith opens! Everything assumes a new aspect! They wave their branches already from afar, those glorious palms around the refreshing fountains of water. And there the children of God then encamp. And, while the bystanders think: "How terrible indeed! how bitterly sorrowful!"—they are not aware of it, they taste as *sweet*, what was *bitter* when it reached the lips.

O, with God or without God, that makes in sickness the bed so altogether different.

## XXVIII

# *"That I May Refresh Myself Before I Go Hence"*

## A LAST CONSCIOUS MOMENT

THE secret hope almost every child of God cherishes on his last sick-bed to make good much of his spiritual negligence, and to die in close nearness to God, as a rule, ends in bitter disappointment.

This hope falls away altogether with all those, who are suddenly taken away out of this life; something by no means of rare occurrence. Whether an accident cuts off our life, or a stroke overtakes us, or a sudden paralysis arrests the action of the heart and makes one stop breathing.

But even when God the Lord allows His child a gentler transition, and even though sickness slowly creeps upon us, which binds us weeks and sometimes months to the sick-bed, yet with such lingering illness you find little of spiritual freshness and succulence; and if from a slow going you hoped to carry away a rich edification for your own soul, in most instances you are deceived.

Surely, there are such soul-exalting, God glorifying sick-beds; and it has happened more than once, that on his last sick-bed a person was permitted, as a witness and prophet of the Lord in the circle of his family to finish a spiritual work. A deathbed as of Jacob has been seen also among Christians.

But he who deems this to be the rule, is mistaken. This is rather highly exceptional.

And when you think of the numbers of those who formerly companied with you spiritually and have since departed, you will mostly find that they were taken away without much spiritual light shining out from their deathbed.

At one time, because they did not expect that this sickness would be unto death. Then again, because the plague that was upon them, dulled their spirit; sometimes removing all clearness from the consciousness. And also at times, because, however baffling it may seem, shortly before their departure there come to many of God's children, bitter darkening and temptation.

Whether in such moments we have to reproach ourselves with respect to this, is a question which every child of God has to decide in his own conscience.

It can also go on altogether outside of our guilt.

The Lord can bring upon us so violent a plague, terrifying our whole being and benumbing our mind in anxiety and pain, that it goes on altogether outside of our soul. And also the darkening and temptation, as Job's example shows, can be a Divinely intentioned trial of our faith.

Yet let no one be overconfident about this; for the cases are not infrequent, that the powerlessness of our faith in such moments is bitter fruit of lack of faith's operation, if not of consenting to sin against God, when we were in health.

So when the bustle of ordinary activities falls away, and diversion ceases, and our soul is thrown back upon herself, all the sinful of our past thrusts itself upon us with overwhelming force; and woe to him who then has no unshakable faith, firm as a rock in the atoning power of the blood of his Savior.

He who then does not positively know and see, that God has cast *all* his sins in the depth of the sea, but has them for his own account, suffers such unbearable remorse and such mortal anxiety.

For surely judgment comes, and for him who is about to die it stands so close at the door.

Then the soul bows itself down under it, and it is only divine compassion that in such dreadful moments can liberate the soul from the bands of death and hell.

BUT however every one personally may stand with his guilt before God, it is certainly wrong when on our sick-bed, that threatens to become our deathbed, the need of glorifying God before our dying, does not become a burden of prayer.

See it in the case of David.

He lay prostrate with a deadly disease; the plague of a serious, dangerous sickness had come upon him; and spiritually he felt himself languid and useless.

He could not battle it.

The force of the disease was too overwhelming, and listless as a log he lay upon his sick-bed.

But, however benumbed and clouded he felt himself to be, there rested him still this one thing, that this miserable, spiritual barrenness was an hindrance to him, and that he thirsted, before dying to have at least a few brief moments, in which the violence of the plague would abate, spiritual self-perception would return, and he could refresh himself preparatory to commending his soul into God's hand.

So he came to pray; and as he prayed tears ran down his face, and then he cried: "Hear my prayer, O Lord, and give ear unto my cry; hold not thy peace at my tears: O, my God, turn thee away from me, that I may refresh myself, before I go hence, and be no more." (Ps. 39, 12 Dutch version).

OF course this prayer of David must not be misunderstood.

It was in no wise an exclamation of unbelief, after the manner of Job's wife, to curse God before he died. The whole 39th psalm shows this differently. Everything in this psalm is the longing of a worn-out and desolate soul after the living God.

But David realized that God was in the plague; that this violent sickness came not upon him by chance, but of God; that in that plague God Himself distressed him; and for this reason he supplicated: Turn thee as the reproving God *externally* away from me, and as the spiritual Comforter come *internally* to me.

And neither will it do to suggest the question, whether indeed David believed in a life after this life, because he said: "before I go hence *and be no more*"; for see, just before this goes the testimony, that even as his fathers he had been a *stranger* and a *sojourner*, which of itself includes the confession of the heavenly fatherland.

No, what this servant of God supplicated was, not to die like a dog; but that before the end came, he might have a moment of relief, before dying to be permitted to refresh himself, and so with clear, bright consciousness of faith to go into eternity.

So in this prayer speaks energy of faith, and in our serious sicknesses this is what we also have to learn from David.

A child of God must *never* give up; but, however violent the plague becomes, always struggle in against it with the elasticity of his spiritual life.

Not as though in himself he would have a certain provision of strength, to keep it up till the end. Faith never knows of anything except weaknesses, that in those weaknesses the power and the work of the Holy Spirit may become manifest.

But it makes all the difference, whether in such moments you let go of the Holy Ghost, or whether inwardly you hold yourself fast to Him.

And this difference you see so frequently.

You find those who lie down upon their sick-bed like a log, and, if they do complain, only complain of what ails their body. But for the rest they have given up. They are indeed willing that one should pray for them, but they no longer pray themselves. They simply undergo what God puts upon them. There is no more effort in their faith, to harness the sinew of faith. Of the glory of the work of the Mediator they see nothing more. Everything about them has become barren and dead. And so the days and nights go by, till finally it goes to death with them.

This is sinning upon one's deathbed.

There is something in this of denial of Christ.

And that this is not necessary, yea, except in times of unconsciousness, is *never* necessary, is shown not only by David, but has equally well been evident with many a person bitterly afflicted and severely plagued, who in the face of everything, and underneath it all, never let go his Pniel, and with heroic courage of faith held on to the uttermost.

Then it was mostly observed, that this heroism of faith inworked upon the body and silenced complaint of pain, in quiet patience to endure, what had to be suffered; and, though all the waves and billows went over him, he yet raised up the head again from out those dreadful waves, until it was enough, and the Lord made an end of it, and God's angels rejoiced, and they who loved him and at his deathbed wept because of their sorrow, yet also thanked God, that they had witnessed *this power of faith* again.

## XXIX

# *"What Is the Measure of My Days?"*

### THOU TOO MUST DIE

TRANSITORINESS is an easily spoken word, and the thought, expressed therein, is by no one contradicted. But how long it takes, before you apply this transitoriness to yourself, and indeed begin to exist to yourself and before your God as a *transient creature*.

All men are mortal, this was taught you already at school, but what boy, as he sees this in writing, thinks for one moment that this includes him. And this not because no children die. Rather mortality among little ones is greater than among adults. But a child does not grasp this. He looks on. He sees the dear little corpse, and will weep honest tears, but, no sooner has he gone away from it, than your boy plays again and romps, and lives as though he had seen no death.

And he who thinks, that this thoughtlessness occurs only with our little ones, thereby shows, that he neither knows his environment, nor his own heart.

The fact cannot be denied, that, however dreadful death may be, nothing is so fleeting and quickly cursory, as the impression, which the dying of one of our own and the sight of a corpse makes.

For one moment we are moved; we come together and mourn; our dead is carried out to the grave; and then we go into mourning; but long before the time for mourning is ended, life has resumed its ordinary course, and it happens but all too frequently, that almost no more word is said about our dead.

Sometimes this is different. There are cases of death, wherewith so terribly much went into the grave, and which brought about so great a change in the life of those who remained behind, that a long time all of life holds in memory the departure of him who passed away.

But, even then it is ever yet the love or the need that operates after, and also this has nothing in common with the application of the transitoriness *to ourselves*.

DAVID too was troubled by this.

Through what vicissitudes of life and dangers of death had not this son of Jesse passed. How many had not fallen by his sword and been struck down by his side! How frequently he had been in danger of death! How oftentimes the dark shadow of death in battle had passed over him!

And still David was not able sufficiently to realize that he himself was a "transitory creature."

He well knew, that no one escapes death. He by no means denied, that his way also would end with the grave. And even that he hoped for a very long life, is nowhere evident.

But what he missed, what he was not sufficiently aware of in his own soul's perception, was the sense, the inner and continuous conviction, that he himself was but a *transitory creature* before his God.

Even when in serious illness he lay upon the sick-bed, or when dangers of death surrounded him, it was ever yet as though the sense of transitoriness would not take hold of him.

And this troubled him. He felt that in this his position was false. And therefore he prayed, that as a special grace his God would teach *him how transitory he was*.

And to learn this, he prayed in Psalm 39: "Lord, make me to know mine end, *and the measure of my days, what it is*."

To this teaching every child of God ought to accustom himself.

Not to desire a revelation, whereby we might foretell the year of our death, and like Hezekiah calculate, that we still have so and so many years before us.

That would lead to the very opposite idea.

No, what we have to make our own is, how short of duration our human life is; how many little flowers wither without unfolding; how many young men and maidens have been cut off just when they were ready to enter upon fullness of life; how many a man is stricken down as an oak, that still exhibited the glory of its foliage; and how beyond sixty-five years of age only five per cent are spared of all that are born of man.

Of every twenty people but one.

Just as is said in Psalm 90, that as a rule seventy years is the uttermost boundary, and that only a few, who are very strong, come to eighty.

And, when one is young, this seems *long*, but how *short*, in reality it is?

Of those sixty or seventy years you sleep away twenty, ten are spent in all sorts of insignificant interests and amidst all sorts of idle chit-chat; another ten are spent at the table; and for real life there rests at most some twenty years, even with those who live longest.

And what is this compared to centuries? To the presently twenty centuries which went since Bethlehem, and the sixty centuries since Adam?

Twenty years to work, even though one lives sixty or seventy years, what is this compared with eternity?

And then one must work eight hours a day, steadily and continuously, and who does this?

You at least did not do this in your tenth year, neither in sickness nor when you were on a journey; and this does not include your Sabbaths.

Accurately counted, a good deal is subtracted from these twenty years, and it is much, when of a life of sixty or seventy years you can count fifteen, in which work is done and something is accomplished.

COMPLAINT here is of no avail.

Our life is no longer than it is. A third must be taken off for sleep. Meals take time, and time the many little activities, connected with the care of the body. Also against sickness we have no safeguard.

But actually the sum of real life comes down to a very small cipher.

Only one in twenty, who fifteen years actually accomplish anything, and the others still far less.

But to be up to this, and then ever yet to live on, *as though it would go on forever,* is a misleading of self that goes too far, an unpardonable shortage of clearness in our own spirit.

With a child of the world this can be understood. When a child of the world dies he loses everything. He is not always afraid of death, some even altogether not. But with death the enjoyment of life ends. And therefore it is so understandable, that a child of the world rather dreams along, in the expectation of after to-day finding yet another day, and for the rest prefers not to think of the future.

But with a child of God this must be otherwise. For him death does not end all, but only after death it really begins.

He *dares* to think of his end, because he knows that this end shall be peace.

For him therefore there is no single reason, why he should always sweetly dream life's dream. He can and must awaken.

Even when he looks into his condition altogether soberly, he is still happy.

AND then there is indeed no thought, which inworks more fruitfully upon his life, than the clear sense, to learn to know himself before God as a *transient creature.*

Nothing so much as this sense stimulates to restless labor.

"Let us work while it is day, the night cometh wherein no man can work."

You are here on earth for a purpose. You have a task. That task must be finished. And then only does God relieve you.

Nothing so much makes generous and loose from earthly goods.

Nothing of what your hand acquired, follows you in the grave. Naked you came from your mother's womb, and naked you return into the grave. You take nothing with you.

Nothing impels you so strongly to hold yourself fast to your God, since He alone is mighty to maintain you as a transient creature, and when it is done here, with eternal arms of compassion to bear you up in eternal existence.

This transitory life, and that eternal, that follows after, is such a powerful stimulus, not to value too highly what is before one's eyes, and to reach out after the crown, that sparkles of invisible diamonds.

"Transitory," and if then you still desire to live, and know that the everlasting is only with your God, then that same sense drives you so mightily, so restlessly on toward the Eternal, and you feel so much more deeply than otherwise, what it says, that He *the Eternal*, is the only One *not* transitory, He Who alone has *immortality*.

And therefore, it is well with you, when the Holy Spirit leads you into this thought, imprints it deeply in your soul, and so penetrates you with the same, that the breath of your life is no more a fruitless hoping, but is in unison with the reality which is hard, and yet so *glorious*.

## XXX

# "Behold, the Judge Standeth Before the Door"

### THE JUDGE STANDETH BEFORE THE DOOR

ALREADY the single fact, that there is *a Judge*, sifts before the conscience guilt from innocence.

See, there are two, one of which *has* oppressed his neighbor and the other *was* oppressed by his neighbor, and now the oppressor boasts of what he gained, and the oppressed moans and complains and feels aggrieved by what was done to him.

And now there is mention of the Judge. The report went abroad of the committed wrong. It penetrated to the place of judgment. It came to the ears of *the Judge*.

So he mingles himself therein; and both persons, the oppressor and the oppressed, are summoned to the seat of judgment. But now think, with what opposite feelings, under what altogether different impression the two make their appearance there.

That there is still *a judge*, that this judge gives a sign of life, that this judge will pronounce judgment, is to the oppressed a cause of *joy*, as though his burden was already removed from his shoulders and the wrong, done him, is scarcely any more felt. But it operates upon the oppressor altogether differently. He feels *troubled* by it. For him it makes an end of his sinful pride. To him that judge is an evil appearance, that haunts him, and whom he so gladly would wish to be far distant.

Were there no judge, the oppressor would have remained jubilant and the oppressed a complainant in his misery. But now that there is a judge, and that that judge will do right, it is the turn of the oppressor, to be in trouble and distress, and the oppressed and sufferer of wrong gets oil of gladness for ashes.

Yea, more still, already the prospect, that the judge would concern himself in it, has given the evil oppressor anticipatory anxiety; and, on the other hand, the glorious prospect, that the judge would repair what was done amiss, has comforted the oppressed in the midst of his trouble and has held his hand back from revenge.

A judge: that is a moral power for the conscience and in life, which by the single fact already, that it exists and presently shall operate, holds back so much evil in its birth, tempers it in its execution and robs it of its malicious self-complacency; while, on the other hand, it alleviates the pain of oppression, lessons the grief of him who has been put in the wrong, offers comfort to him, that is cast down, shields from embitterment of soul and seeking of retaliation.

LET therefore the thought of *the* Judge of all judges remain unweakened in the conscience of our Christian nations, and above all see to it, that you do not take away the remembrance of *that judge* from the consciousness of our race. O, truly, if you are God's child, He is your Father, and Love is His nature, "merciful and gracious and of great goodness" is His Name.

But still, when the Lord God proclaimed His holy, glorious Name so majestically to the ear of Moses, His servant, He immediately added thereto, as equally truly belonging to His Name: *"Who will by no means clear the guilty,"* even as the Our Father would have been unthinkable without the prayer to the Judge: "Forgive us our trespasses."

Freely preach therefore the love and the riches of the mercies of the Lord as broadly, as generously, as aboundingly as lies within your power, but do not preach it falsely, do not cut the life-nerve of it, lift not out of it the animation and the energy.

Formerly every one's conscience still knew, that that very Father in the heavens, even as every one's father on earth, in His Fatherhood, and in virtue of His Fatherhood, is at the same time Judge.

Without that background of the Judge one could not think of the Father in the heavens.

Father in the heavens was then no term yet of emotion, no sentimental conception, no sound of weak good nature, but still entered really and truly into the ear with the full, rich, deep sense, which by nature lies in that holy name of Father.

But now this has been meddled with. The "Judge" has been left out, passed by in silence, presently antagonized. Judge, no, such the Father in the heavens is no more!

In the heavens and on the throne of glory there is no holy, separating and sifting energy carrying things through with a strong hand, but merely a weak goodheartedness, muddling everything together, to all things closing the eye.

So the evil conscience wanted it. And philosophy replied: It is quite possible. And misled by her sweet whistling a false theology also in the pulpit has fed this false representation.

And so in many churches one now almost never hears a mention of the Judge.

There are no exhalations save ever and again that impotent, pithless, creative of nothing good-heartedness or rather yet good-naturedness.

The rich, glorious Father-love of God, the fullness of His impenetrable compassion and fathomless mercifulness has been reduced to a superficial, shallow, soulless compassionateness.

Result of this is, that now the masses almost never more think of that Judge, neither concern themselves about Him, nor on His account refrain from anything.

Of which in turn the still sadder result is, that the sense of guilt grows ever more faint and haughtiness assumes ever more irremedial proportions.

And why then should one still seek *the Redeemer?*

O, he who is not bowed down under the weight of sin and guilt, and never was weary or heavy laden, does not thirst after the sweet of atonement.

A rough drunkard, a wicked blasphemer can still be induced to turn to Jesus, but no more the rank and file of people.


THAT dreadful evil of nerveless preaching ought to be arrested.

*The Judge* must be counted with again in our life. The thought of the Judge must be valid again in our consciousness. We ourselves must listen again and make our children listen to that dreadful apostolic warning: *Behold, the judge standeth before the door!* (James 5, 9).

The moment, you really believe this, you do no sin; as no thief would steal, if he saw the judge himself standing at the door.

For among people the sometimes still bitter experience weakens confidence, that a judge will judge righteously; or will merely do so by half measure; sometimes even directly violating right.

But with *the* Judge there is no such cause for weakening. *That* Judge does not close the all-seeing eye to any matter whatever. Nothing escapes His observation. He needs no informer and no witness. Every evil action lies naked and open before Him, with Whom we have to do.

Moreover every one's conscience knows well, that this Judge adways doeth right and never, never violates *Right*.

With this Judge everything that could weaken falls away. He shines in the full majesty of the Justice, which condemns *all* sin and delivers every one who is oppressed.

Place therefore your own soul, place your own environment, place the church of God, place country and people again before the Judge, and an altogether different spirit will pervade our heart and the circle of our life.

The enervated conscience will become sinewy again.

God's children in particular will be troubled again in the face of sin still cherished.

There will be trembling in souls again before the living God.

And also, there will comforting again flow out to those that are oppressed; in that prospect of coming justice courage and strength will revive again, for a time to bear wrong and injustice; and in the face of all injustice and tyranny, even as our fathers, we shall learn, gladly and ecstatically to look forward to the day of judgment and of retribution, in which the Lord, the righteous Judge, shall destroy "His and our enemies."

This now one no longer dares to do. This is deemed loveless. And one forgets, that nothing is more loveless, than to estrange our generation from the Judge and thereby from *Justice;* thus to deaden the *sense of guilt;* and by this deadening of the sense of guilt to keep souls away from *the Savior* of their soul.

And therefore, let the Judge stand again before the door. Not only actually. For this He doeth anyway. But clearly before our consciousness.

The fruit of it will be so glorious!

So refreshing for the tepidness of the spiritual atmosphere around us.

## XXXI

## *"Made an End of Commanding His Sons"*

### AROUND OUR DEATHBED

A *dyingbed* in the rich, full sense of the word is becoming more and more rare.

In former times it was gloried in. And when at advanced age father or mother went into eternity, after upon their deathbed they had still cared for their children, and had exhorted and admonished them, and, before their latest breath, had gloried in the grace of God and the peace of their Savior, such a dyingbed left behind an indelible impression. Such a dyingbed edified more than ten sermons. So one had seen father pass away, so gloriously mother had died, and since then the desire has been awake in the soul, in such blessed peace oneself to be permitted to enter upon eternity.

We do not say, that such pious and instructive dyingbeds do no more occur at all, but yet, one hears less of them.

This is owing in part to the nature of the disease, for he who is taken with a shock or stricken with a stupefying illness, in most cases dies unconsciously.

In part also to the fact, that our sick are left in uncertainty, whether indeed it comes to dying.

And, alas, there is much guilt also with the less pious manner of family life; with the weaker desire to bear witness; and not being sufficiently animated with respect to eternity.

Our present-day life is so overwhelmingly rich in impressions, that already thereby our life has lost in depth.

A strong development in luxuriant growth of leaf; but in the root backward.

So one lives *strenuously*, but not *profoundly*.

One accustoms himself all too much to *gliding* through life, and so in the end one *glides* out from this life into the dreadful eternity.

OF Jacob's dyingbed, which remains the example for the dying of God's saints in all ages, three things are recorded.

First that he gave his sons commandments. Then, that he gathered up his feet into the bed. And third, that he yielded up the ghost, and was gathered unto his people (Gen. 49, 33).

Consider for a moment this first thing by itself alone: Jacob, the old patriarch, before he parted from his children, *gave his sons commandments.*

What divine restfulness and sacred peace there must have been in the old patriarch, that in that last hour he was almost not at all concerned with himself, but almost exclusively with his children.

How deeply he saw into the different characters of each of his children, and, under higher inspiration, what rich prophecy he was able to prophesy, even with respect to their descendants.

And yet, before we come to this, there is still something else, and you do well exclusively to consider that: *He gave commandments.*

Even as Jesus said in the parable: *"Set thine house in order,* for this night thy soul shall be required of thee" (Luke 12, 20).

And even this so many no more do.

Even of aged people who died, you hear it again and again, that they made no arrangements whatever; that no one knows, how they would have their effects disposed of; and that so their heirs must act in the dark.

In most cases a meaningless testament was made, when they married. And ever since they have lived along, as though from year to year this goodly, kindly life would endlessly go on.

Life was not lived thoughtlessly; but one lived year in year out, without ever a serious thought about one's demise.

And so wife and children often stand at the bier, not knowing what to do; themselves in most cases having no knowledge of affairs; and so the real disposition passes over into the hands of a lawyer, who settles everything.

AND this is not permissible.

Up to your latest breath you are a responsible person, and if you are the head of your family, and father of children and steward of certain goods, and your own have been accustomed during your lifetime to lean and be dependent upon you, you may not at your dying so suddenly take that staff out of their hand.

From of old one heard of all sorts of testaments.

Of a testament of course concerning property one leaves behind, but also concerning so much more.

In such a testament one made confession once more of his faith and of the hope of glory, in which one died. In such a testament father gave advice and admonition to the children, which he left behind. And if he had been engaged in matters of State or Church or other public affairs, not infrequently there was found in such a testament still further instruction or disposition of how to act.

And even regarding his funeral and the spot where one desired to rest until the last day, such a testament often gave helpful hints.

And of course, he who wrote his testament in such a frame of mind, did not forget the mercies; and if he had abundant means, and wife and children were well provided for, he remembered poor members of the family, the poor of God's church, or all sorts of institutions, which aimed at the glory of God.

THE frame of mind, expressed herein, was no mystery.

From such calm and quiet setting in order of one's house it was evident, that one had *counted* with dying, and had not ignored the saying of Jesus, "that He would come as a thief in the night."

He who so departs, had made himself conversant with the matter while he was still in life. With the dying of others he had thought about his own dying. And had not found it in conflict with an healthy rule of life, in the full strength of life to hold death before his eyes.

It was still understood what is said in the Psalms: *Death beckons every hour.*

Not that therefore one was sated with life or tired

of life. Far less than now suicide was then heard of. And the disposition of spirit on the part of the aged was far more courageous and vigorous than now.

Even young people and children were then fond of old people; found them interesting; and were glad to be with them.

Only it was more the natural life of a man, who knows that he is a pilgrim here on earth, and that the real object of his existence is *outside* of this earth.

A pilgrim's consciousness, which did not render him indifferent to the things of this earth, for before he died, he set in order, also his house.

BUT yet, stronger still than this setting in order of his house, there interests you in Jacob that giving of commandments *to his sons*.

Jacob in dying is *engaged with his children*.

Those children are the continuation of his life, when he shall be no more upon this earth.

And though you grant, that by prophetic inspiration Jacob was able to bear testimony regarding his children in a way, such as is impossible to you, who do not have this inspiration, yet this prophetic inspiration did not go outside of the natural knowledge, which he had of each one of his children.

Jacob had evidently studied his children. He had watched their doings and their ways. He had so entered into their characters that from their characters he could estimate their natures.

And on his dyingbed he calls them all around him.

"Come together," says he, "ye sons of Jacob, and listen to Israel, your father."

He was *their father*.

He had generated them after more than the flesh. And as *their father* he wanted also in his dying still to do his duty by his children.

And now he does not spare them.

The evil characters he brands in the presence of them all; for also dying must be holy, and in no tenderness of heart may sin be condoned.

But yet in what he says to each one of his sons there speaks *fatherly seriousness*. It is as though, before he goes hence, he wants to let a beam of light shine on the path of every one of them, that head for head they shall walk their path with more self-consciousness.

In that address of the dying Jacob there is such a wealth of fatherly tenderness.

That aged patriarch has been more busy with his children than with his money and goods.

And also in his dying there is no complaint of pain or inconvenience of his own, but the future of his children holds all the attention of the dying saint.

How altogether different from what now you often see.

Our age, in which money is so highly esteemed, has choked so much tenderness.

And yet faith must not drift away with this.

God's people must not yield to this.

And as need is the more imperative, to separate ourselves in our own circle, and also for our children to seek a life-circle of their own, so also must dying among us become less conformable again to the world.

For that is the real thing.

The world dies differently from the way in which God's saints die.

And where the world tries to entice us even on our dyingbed to her side, it is the calling of the people of God, at least on the dyingbed to exclude the world.

In your dying at least you must be a child of your God.

## XXXII

## *"Death, Where Is Thy Sting?"*

### THE STING OF DEATH

In healthy, young days, when nothing ails us, and laughter is scarcely absent from our lips, one can sometimes speaks so light-heartedly of death.

Not just *to mock* with death; for that does not occur in our circles; but yet to treat of death, as though you thought in yourself: "Well yes, that is still a long way off. So bad and dreadful death will not be. Moreover death has nothing to do with me yet. It is by no means yet my turn!"

But when serious sickness takes hold of you, and distressed and gasping for breath, as the sickness grows worse you lie in bed, and those around you in manner and look betray uneasiness, and the doctor does not conceal the fact, "that you are not altogether out of danger," then that thought of death at once makes an altogether *different impression* upon you.

What thus far was little more to you than a sound and a name, what at most sounded as a somber tone in your ear, or wakened in you the transient idea of something shrill and shivery, and which therefore immediately you banished again from your soul and mind, appears then at once before you as a dreadful reality; as a power that steals upon you; yea, as a menacing danger, from which by no manner of struggling you can withdraw yourself.

*Perchance* you may yet recover. You still *pray* yourself, and dear ones pray for and with you. Also medical science does what it can.

But still it remains critical. The pulsebeat far too quick. The heat of the blood far too high. The trouble within not arrested but progressing.

O, you still *may* come out of it. All hope is not yet gone. But it is also possible that it takes a *different* turn, and that presently the thread of your life is cut off.

And then it goes sometimes painfully fast. Before the week is yet ended, not merely dead, but sometimes already put away in the grave.

In such days, you get to see *death* in the face. Every time again involuntarily you think of it. Not that superstitiously you represent him to yourself as a skeleton with skull and sickle; but you realize, that about that mysterious death there is something dreadful; that same death, that from righteous Abel on has made every child of man pay the bitter toll, that tore away from the circle of family and friends so much that was dear, and now presses himself upon you, makes close approach to you, lays the hand upon your shoulder, as though to say to you, that you must hasten, for that your hour is at hand.

And when for the first time you perceive this in all its seriousness, a shudder passes through your soul, and a shiver through the body. You feel the chill of the shadow of death already passing over you, and darkness attending his approach.

For though on the field of battle the hero truly at times *seeks* death, and at the stake martyr after martyr has *laughed* him in the face; yet battle-field and stake are something so altogether different from a sick-room with all the anguish of broken physical strength.

The hero and the martyr are still in perfect health.

Death has made no approach yet in the body. Death still stands over against them. And for the sake of the banner of their *heavenly* King, courageously and with despisal of death they rather die than surrender that banner.

But when in weakness and distress you face your end, there is no more strength left in you. Nothing that holds you up or stimulates your ardor. Still a few days perhaps, and so quietly, so forsakenly, so imperceptibly you pass away.

AND then you stand before a riddle, before the question, what then shall it be?

You are going to die, but what is it to die?

What will you then feel, what perceive, what become aware of? That tearing apart of soul and body, will it be distress, or excruciating pain?

You ask, and, alas, no one has an answer; for no one who died has ever told us, how it was to him in his dying.

The whole transition from this life to the other side of eternity is a world of riddles.

For some were indeed seen dying in conditions of terrible distress, when the death-struggle seemed almost endless, while others slept away so gently and calmly, that it was difficult to believe, that that was dying.

But what avails this observation? Who can tell, what, when the utterance of life went from him, went on in the hidden parts of that dying man between soul and body, and in his soul?

Surely, with a shock or paralysis of heart death can enter in so suddenly and so painlessly, that neither our eye nor ear observe any suffering. But is everything said with this? Is what we see the real, actual dying?

And so we go on asking, but no answer comes, and the thought, that now it comes to your turn, continues to harass you. For when it comes, how then will it be with you?

SCRIPTURE speaks respecting death of a *sting*, as the apostle exclaims: "O death, where is thy sting? O grave, where is thy victory" (I Cor. 15, 55).

The image thus of a *poisonous* monster, that not merely attacks you, but stings with his sting, and poisons by the same. Something like as dragons were represented, and as there are serpents still.

And by that poisonous sting, that horribleness of death is imaged.

Not merely that he takes your life, but in addition to this that poisonous thrust with the sting, that when you are in his power, when you are dead, he may poison your existence on the other side of the grave.

And this must not be passed by lightly, for in this imagery there is truth. Death is unclean; death is poisonous; and he who remains in the power of death, is prey to joyless terror and never ending distress of soul.

Dying itself is not the worst. That only *comes afterward*, when you have died, and they lay you out in your death garment, and carry you to God's-acre.

Dying itself is merely *going through* the gate of death; but then you arrive in the valley of the shadows of death, and then in his fortress; and there dread and terror shall take hold of you; with no other prospect than to wait age upon age, until Christ returns upon the clouds, and then yourself to go into judgment, and then with everything demoniac to be driven out into still greater terror. Into that horror, of which Jesus said: "There shall be weeping and gnashing of teeth."

It all depends therefore upon this: Whether, *before death takes hold of you,* you can break that sting of death.

If you can do that, you die as a Christian, as a child of God, as one redeemed. Then you die like a S. Paul, who betimes, before it was too late, had broken that sting of death, and now already long in advance, jubilant and laughing death in the face, exclaimed: "O death, where is thy sting? You no longer have it. And therefore you are no more to me the king of terror!"

Thus you realize, if once that sting, that poisonous sting of death is broken, then death has become something altogether different. So long as a wasp has her sting, you flee from her; but when the sting is removed, you play with the wasp as with a fly.

Death *without* sting, *without* poisonous sting is a messenger of God, who comes to fetch you away; who in the Name of the Lord divests you of your body; admits you as a liberated soul through the gate of Eternity, to be nearer to your God and your Savior, than ever you were able to be here, and, without sorrow and without sin, to tarry in that spiritual separation, till the light dawns of the eternal morning, and Christ comes upon the clouds, and clothes you with a more glorious body, and deluges you with everlasting glory.

Death *with* his sting is terrible. Then you are gone. Then in death there are bands of hell and of eternal torment.

But if death *has lost* his sting, then at once all terror is gone.

Then there are those who have longed for death, because death alone was able to bring them to be eternally with their God.

ONLY make no mistake.

There are a kind of Catechism-Christians, who briefly reason like this: "Christ is risen from the dead. By that Resurrection Christ has broken the sting of death. Thus there is no more sting to death. And I can confidently fall asleep!"

As though there ever could flow any joy from mere *reasoning*.

No, also after Jesus' resurrection, death has *retained* his poisonous sting. Think of the many thousands, who *without* faith in Jesus, also after Jesus' resurrection, have become the prey of death.

Even now there die those, to whom in their dying he brings that poisonous sting.

And you say truly, that many thousands have departed, to whom every sting had gone from death, but with all these it was a *personal* act.

When death came *to them,* then, indeed, at once

that sting became inoperative, which still stung others so poisonously.

And so your reasoning from your Catechism avails you nothing.

With you also the question remains, whether, when death comes to you, your faith in Christ is operative, whereby that sting of death is disarmed.

If so, then do not fear.

Then, then alone, but then also *surely*, will your end be *peace*.

## XXXIII

# "At an Hour When Ye Think Not"

## SUDDEN DEATH

Taken deeply psychologically is what the Psalmist says in Psalm 49, 11, of the children of the world: "Their inmost thought is, that their houses shall continue forever, their dwelling places to all generations." And we hasten to add, that by nature God's child also has this trait in common with the child of the world.

A good, substantial house, built upon a foundation, can last for centuries. And when we hear of father and grandfather, who already have lived in that same house; and now we ourselves equally safely live in it, without any crack showing itself in the wall or a tie-beam creaking in the ceiling, then indeed, we too anticipate the future, when our children will take our places in that house, and presently be succeeded by the family, that God will give them.

Especially a countryman feels this strongly, when it is his privilege, from generation to generation, with his family to occupy the old homestead. For, even though changes were put upon the house, that land, that broad ground on which his house stands, and upon which his harvests ripen, and his cattle graze, remains at least always the same, and he cannot imagine, that that ground, those pastures, shall once cease to exist.

You feel this still more strongly of *the city or village,* in which you live. For whether the houses are torn down and new ones built, and sometimes a parcel of ground is expropriated for the sake of a canal or railway, the city itself, the village, in which we live, never passes away. It does not show the slightest token of decay. How in the world would such a city or village ever come to an end?

But strongest of all we have this feeling with respect to *our whole earth.* Though in Scripture we read of great cities like Babylon and Nineveh, which have been levelled to the ground; and though we read of the Holy land, that once flowed with milk and honey, and now is so barren and bald; yet the spot, where Babylon once stood, still lies ever unmoved, and streams of pilgrims still journey to parched Palestine.

Though thus we well know, that *houses* at length are demolished, and *cities* can disappear, and even tracts of ground can sink away by earthquakes, the world itself always remains, so we think, and whatever disappears or goes away, the earth itself remains what it is.

YET Holy Scripture is diametrically opposed to this universal human idea, and tells you, that this earth shall *not* remain as it is; that the whole world shall once be changed; that once time itself shall be no more; and that then comes the consummation of the ages.

And we listen to this. We allow ourselves to be told so. And he who believes, does not contradict it. But yet it does not move us. And we go on living in the idea, as though all things will remain as they now are.

Formerly this was not so. There have ever been times, that it was quite generally believed, that the end of the world was at hand. It was reckoned up to within a year, when the world was to be destroyed. And once accepting this for certain, not a few sold their lands and goods; and spent the money; thinking that a following year, when the world would end, it would be no more good to them.

But just because that "passing away of the world" had so frequently been foretold, and that this prophecy had never been fulfilled, gradually all faith in such prophecies was lost. Soon mockery was made of it. And so gradually the representation came in vogue, as though endlessly, always, things on earth would remain as they now are.

Only in certain circles of God's people reckoning was still made with the positive prophecy of the return of the Lord; even though as a rule it had little influence upon the general mind and general behavior.

And this has lasted, until the crust of the earth began to be examined, and science began to give itself account, of what took place in the heart of the earth.

Then one saw as before his eyes, that this world has by no means always been what it now is; that terrible changes and upturnings have taken place in the crust of the earth; and saw for instance in coal, that great forests, that formerly stood on the surface of this earth, now, deep under ground, have sunken away in mines and are carbonized.

So it was discovered, that our earth inwardly is alive and tosses and ferments. So volcanoes and earthquakes found their natural explanation. But thereby also the insight was reached, that in the future our earth cannot remain what it now is, but soon or late must stiffen in cold or be destroyed in a world conflagration.

This in turn sitmulated students of Scripture. In the circles of God's people another outlook again was obtained upon that world and its future. And now it has come so far, that only the superficial and more dozing than live people still dream of an endless continuance of the world.

He who is up to the times, among the children of God as among the children of the world, now knows, that once all this world shall pass away.

AND yet, though both people of faith and men of science know, that, soon or late, "the fashion of this world passeth away," yet the impression of this conviction is so different with both.

A difference consisting in this, that the man of the world puts this day far off; and the man of faith proclaims: "The day of the Lord is at hand." That the men of science say: "It will last our time," and that in His Word the Lord testifies: "I come as a thief in the night." Or if you will, the rejectors of Scripture measure out the duration of the world by periods of centuries, and that Christ warns us: "Be ye therefore ready also: for the Son of man cometh at an hour when ye think not" (S. Luke 12, 40).

In practical life the results of this difference of viewpoint are incalculable. To one it becomes a rule of life: "Do as though there never comes an end"; and to the other: "Do as though to-morrow the end of the world were at the door."

Just the same difference, that you find with the outlook upon death.

Also with respect to this both the child of God and the child of the world know, that once our life shall end; that from afar or close by already now death awaits us; and that once the grave shall be the resting-place of us all.

But though he knows this, the child of the world says: "Speak not of it." And so death may not be referred to, even when the doctor knows and sees and says, that to-morrow the end comes. While on the other hand the child of God really lives no single day, that he does not think of his end; ever prepares his soul to die; and, especially with serious sickness, turns aside every veil, with clear open eyes to look into eternity.

To some extent you can even say, that the coming of Jesus upon the clouds, and the coming of death, to fetch us away, to God's child is *one* thing; for when we die, to us the end of the world is really already come. For a while that world then withdraws itself from our eyes; and the first moment, after our resurrection, we shall see her again, shall be the *last* moment, at which Christ shall sit in judgment.

Though it be thus ever so true, that we must be pious, not for the sake of death, but for God's sake, yet it is equally certain, that thinking upon death is the great, of God ordered means, to break the overwhelming impression of the power of the world, and to let the impression of the majesty of God inwork the more effectively upon us.

It is no chance, that the hour of our death is so uncertain, and that dying overtakes almost every one *at an hour when he does not think it*.

So God the Lord appointed it *purposely*, thereby

to hold our soul in constant, wholesome tension, and to weaken our boundedness to the world.

And where even this uncertainty of life appeared not strong enough, to make looser that attachment, that cleaving, that boundedness and enslavement to the world, He brings every time again that broad wave-beat of death upon us, which we call *an epidemic*.

That so many more die than at other times.

That so many die at once.

That in every domain the life of princes is cut off like grapes.

Just to impress upon our soul this one reality, that the abiding is not in this world, but in the Lord our God.

And he who is wise takes heed, lest death take him by surprise.

## XXXIV

# "Thrust in Thy Sickle and Reap"

### THRUST IN THY SICKLE AND REAP

EVERYTHING has its appointed time. For everything, to come, is an hour. For every decision, that must come, tarries the exact moment.

This affects us strangely. Not except with difficulty can our indolent spirit enter into that idea of a decisive moment. And yet all creation shows it.

First the plow cuts through the field. Then the sower goes out to sow, and scatters seed in the plowed furrows.

And when God from heaven sends down sunshine and rain, the ground passes into a state of ferment, seed germinates and springs up, and long weeks, long months our eye feasts itself upon that growth and mellowing of the blades. From morning till evening and from evening until morning grain expands therein. And it seems, as though that grain had no other destiny, than to cover that field with waving gold and magically to increase wealth in nature.

And yet, this was merely *appearance*.

For at length the trained eye of the farmer sees, that grain in the ears is *altogether* ripened. And then he observes wind and tide, whether he can count upon dryness of atmosphere. And when the favorable moment is come, his orders go out to his farmhands. And tomorrow, when the sun is but scarcely risen, that field of wheat is doomed to death. That golden yellow grain has for the last time glistened in the sunlight. See, the sickle descends, handled by nimble, agile hand against the bending stalks, and not long, before all the beautiful grain by handfuls lies cast down upon the ground; is presently set up in sheaves; is carried to the threshing-floors; till the orphan and the poor come for the after gleanings. And then nothing remains more save the empty, black, bald field, with its stubble.

Expressive of so much, so deeply significant.

First weeks and months together that quiet, calm, almost perceptible growth and ripening. And then all at once that day of harvest. That sickle thrust into the stalks. And gone is everything that was there.

In that sowing and growing, that ripening and mowing there speaks a voice of God.

His Holy Scripture constantly points to it. Also in the image of ripening clusters turning blue on the vine, till the vine-dresser cuts off the juicy grapes. But by whatever image, it is always again the same thought, first that slow, quiet becoming and expanding, and then suddenly that breach, that consummation, that mowing or that cutting off. Everything moving forward toward an end, until it is reached, and then at once the stroke of the hand of the mower; that fullness of time; that hour when it is done with what *lay behind* and that *something new* takes its beginning and presently begins.

For when the sickle has been thrust in, and every sheaf is brought to the threshing-floor, the *first* process is indeed ended, but equally surely at once a *second* begins. Then the grain is threshed and shaken out; the wheat separated from the chaff; the kernel broken or ground into meal; and so ripens by a new process *bread* that will be food for man; in the human body again by a new process to prosecute another end, and not to rest, till seed scattered by human hands has come back to man and is transposed *into his own blood*.

And all this disposed and appointed and ordained by God Almighty, Who has measured out the time of sowing and the time of reaping. Who imparted to wheat and to yeast the affinity to form dough and bread. And who now follows up that precious bread with His blessing, to transpose it into the component parts of our own blood.

And what then takes place in every process is always *that twofold operation*. First that slow ripening and expanding, and then finally that sudden moment, wherein that ripening and expanding find their consummation and He breaks off what was, in order, from what He makes it undergo, to make the new to sprout.

Always *His* Word, that does not return unto Him void, but doeth that whereunto He sent it. As snow and rain descends the moisture from His treasure chamber. Then the earth drinks it in and soils it. Until in the earth it meets the pregnant grain kernel. This it then makes to swell and burst and to send up a germ. It lets itself be sucked up in the blade. To the ear the moisture penetrates. And when presently the expanded and blessed bread enters into our blood, to strengthen our vital powers, there is always in it yet a drop of that moisture, which God sent out in snow and rain, to give bread to the eater and seed to the sower.

ONE thing especially God's holy Word requires, that in connection with this you should ever hold before your eyes. It wills, that you should consider, how it goes with *all the things around* you, and that it goes the same way *with yourself.*

As those blades sprang up in the field and grew, and presently were harvested away from that field, so also bloom and ripen the children of men on the field of our human life; and for them also comes the hour of consummation, that the sickle descends upon the blades, and the place which they occupied in the field is no more known.

And here too again the selfsame antithesis. First weeks and years together that quiet, steady, seemingly ever continuous ripening and mellowing in the field; and then suddenly that turn in the condition, that thrusting of the sickle into the blades. And then it is ended and the head droops, till presently the place is empty.

An antithesis, a sudden transition, which, however frequently seen, ever yet so surprises us, that almost no one is prepared, when the sickle comes to him. Things seemed to go along so sweetly. So imperceptibly a new part of the way seemed to join itself to the parts already covered. Advance was so gradual, so steady, so lasting. After every evening always again a morning; after every winter again a spring with flowers that opened, and birds, which in the branches sang their song unto God. Ah, why then should there come an end? Why no endless going on?

And yet, that end comes, because God lives and has command over you and makes disposition of you, and because He granted you this quiet growing and expanding, not for the sake of that growing and expanding, but *that there should be an harvest for Him.*

For as the husbandman bides the moment, when that growing shall be ended, and his word to his servants: "Thrust in the sickle and reap" (Rev. 14, 15) can be spoken, so tarries and bides God the Lord with every one of His children of men, ever anticipating that appointed moment, that fixed hour, when ripening shall be ended, and the fruit of all His care, which He expended upon you, can be carried into His Kingdom.

Your world is for Him. It is His field, in which all that blossoms and ripens, ripens and blossoms for Him, that He, the Lord of the harvest, may also from *this* field obtain His harvest.

And all the days of your life He takes notice of you, looking forward to that moment of consummation, when the fruit of His labor comes to Him.


O, BLESSED is he, whom it may befall in that hour of harvest, that, presently purified by the winnow, he may prove a precious fruit from the field of the world for the Lord his God.

Then the sickle mows not to destroy, but gathers in for God's eternal Kingdom. Then there has been a growing and blooming, then there was a ripening and expanding. And the object was attained: the consummated and perfected fruit, which then enters upon a new future, after new ordinances to serve God the Lord in His holy counsel.

Let every man take heed.

The sickle, that mows the full ears of grain, also mows away the weeds that have sprung up, and also mows away the empty or scorched blades, from which no grain shall dance upon the threshing floor.

Then it did not go *according to* God's Word, but *against* God's Word.

Then it was no growing but degenerating, no ripening and expanding but emaciating and shrinking.

And when then the day of harvest comes, the judgment is so inevitable.

The winnow, shaken by God's holy hand, separates so irrevocably the *wheat* from the *chaff*.

# "He Gathered Up His Feet Into the Bed"

## THE DYINGBED

Also in your dying, and in the sickness that precedes it, you may not cast away your human dignity.

*Man* the Lord created you; and man must suffer differently from a beast, and die differently than a beast dies. The preacher truly testifies, that dying itself is common to you and your dog, but Scripture shows you already in Jacob, the patriarch, what even in that dying extremity the faith of God's child can do.

Jacob was old and sick, and felt that his end was near. He lay at the gate of death. And seeing that gate already opening, he called his sons to his bedside.

And when they came, he did not helpless and breathless remain lying on his bed. No, it says: "Then Israel strengthened himself, and sat upon the bed" (Gen. 48, 2). This means to say, that he put his legs out of bed and on the edge of the bed sat upright.

And yet Jacob did not die young.

He was an old man of one hundred forty-seven years.

Evidently he was rather inclined to remain lying down. He was exhausted and at the limit of his strength. Sitting upright cost him violent exertion. For it reads, that he had to *strengthen* himself for it, i.e., take hold of himself and do his uttermost best.

But he did it.

He was not going to be dragged off as a prey by death, but would die as a hero of faith.

And when the fairly long address to his sons was ended, he himself gathered, so we read, his feet into the bed again, drew them together, and thus yielded up the ghost (Gen. 49, 33).

SUCH exhibition of heroism in human dying occurs also *outside* of faith and in opposition to faith.

A heathen emperor of Rome, at the approach of his end when death was already upon him, stood up against a wall, and refused to go to bed, for, said he, an emperor must die standing.

This was *outside* of faith. From pride.

But sometimes also in opposition to faith there is such heroic dying.

At least the writer of this has witnessed, how up to a few minutes before his death a ruffian stood up in his bed, raving and cursing against the Most High God and exhausting his last vital strength in rage against the Almighty.

And this should not astound you.

Satan works with no other powers than God works with, but he turns them into their opposite. *Hate* in its kinds is as strong as *love*.

The only difference is, that he who before dying strengthens himself in his faith, himself is weak, and in his weakness lets the strength of Christ perfect itself.

Therefore as an hero of faith he does not struggle against death. He does not resist. When death comes, it is to him an ambassador on the part of Christ. And when his hour is come, he walks through the valley of the shadow of death, and the rod and the staff of the Lord comfort him.

That Roman emperor allowed himself standing up to be vanquished. That ruffian fought death, till he was felled by it. But a child of God follows willingly, knowing that death also is a creature, that without God's will can neither stir nor move.

YET one should not be heartless here in his judgment.

Sometimes there are sick, who are going to die, and cannot thus strengthen themselves. Such is the case with sicknesses that stupefy, or which by high fever send the blood to the head and render one delirious. Such is the case in terribly exhausting sicknesses, whereby one loses all control of the body, and finally half-unconsciously drops off, and is gone, before one of the bystanders can know it. Also sudden death by shock or paralysis of the heart excludes every possibility of clear, elastic, heroic and animated dying.

Had Jacob passed away of such a disease, he too would not have died so bravely.

Thus let us distinguish well. There is dying and dying. And no standard common to all can be set up.

But this lessens in nothing the claim, that he who can die bravely and in the power of faith, *must* also do it.

*Must* do this for himself, for his loved ones and for his God.

Also in dying you shall not be merely passive, but in holier sense be active.

In dying, too, you have a *task*, a *calling*, a sacred

*duty* to fulfill. Your last piece of work on earth. But a task, at your account; for which all your life long you have to prepare yourself; and of which you shall give account to the Judge of your heart and your thoughts.

This task touches also *your loved ones*.

Your death must leave behind a fruit for them. Presently your love can no more benefit them, but can still do so in your dying. For the impression of an heroic and believing deathbed always leaves behind a glorious preachment. An impression not easily wiped out.

And thus likewise you have to die honorably *for God's sake*.

For God's honor, over against Satan and his satellites, hangs by it; hangs by it, that also in the dying of His child the power of faith be manifest.

AND whether you can do anything for this?

Yea, surely you can.

Learn it of Jacob. First he *strengthened* himself, let down his feet from the bed, sat upright, leaning on his staff, and with animation addressed his children. And when that task was ended, he did not call for help, and they did not put him to bed, but he himself drew his feet into the bed and placed them together upon the couch, from which he would be carried out to Canaan.

And how Jacob could do this? He, the dying man!

Evidently because he did not put up his faith as in a sheath on the wall, but used it to the end as a weapon, to exhibit hero courage.

Yet Jacob could not do this at once.

If long years before his death Jacob had accustomed himself, to act in times of accident or sickness cowardly and soulless, this wrong would have avenged itself in his dying.

Power of faith is no imagination, but a motion of soul, which expresses itself in will-power and elasticity; and only as fruit of steady exercise of faith, an exercise that steeled the will, such a royal dyingbed was granted the old patriarch.

*Dying* hangs together with your *living*.

When in life you have accustomed yourself, to go out of the way for the body; to have the body dominate you; and cowardly to yield to every emotion in the body; how in the world, when finally the whole body must go under, will you in dying heroically maintain your stand?

Therefore the dyingbed stands immediately related to the sickbed.

One is *under* his sickness, and the other *above* it. This is because, with spirit- and faith-power one resists the stupefaction and exhaustion of the disease, while the other holds himself limp and cowardly, and at once lets himself be overwhelmed by the effect of his sickness.

This difference you see already in your children, when they suffer pain. Then one succumbs and shrinks back from it and sets up a great crying, while the other child holds himself in leash and exhibits courage.

With the child, even as with the man, this can be over-boldness and insensibility springing from the same. Nerves also with one are far stronger than with the other. And then, indeed, this must be led into better paths.

For that same Jacob who so died, was the counterpart of insensibility, and cried like a child when he heard of Joseph's death, and wept when he saw Joseph again.

But the reverse in your child demands equal leading. Oversensitiveness is sin, and *must* be fought against. It is unworthy of a man. And as often as pain or distress or suffering of sickness overtakes us, *the man* in man must be evident; he may not throw himself away; and if he is a child of God, even though Satan beats him with fists, he must be able to do all things through Christ Who giveth him strength.

So every fault in your training avenges itself still upon your dyingbed. For on the development of courage in suffering, hangs the honor of your faith.

But also the example of your environment operates so mightily upon you.

Just because so few patriarchical dyingbeds are witnessed, every idea is lost of the calling, which awaits us still in our dying.

You see people around you ever so greatly engrossed with the service of the body, to feed it, to clothe it, to ornament it, to bandage it when it incurred maiming; and of the care for feeding, clothing and ornamenting the *spirit*, the *soul* within, you observe so little.

This weakens. It extinguishes the high-spiritedness of faith, it quells faith in the power of faith. And so the impression of the material becomes so gigantically great, and the impression of the spiritual so dwarfishly small.

Then one no longer dares with his faith to resist that gigantic power.

And so there are more and more who succumb, till it pleases God to raise up again certain heroes *also in this matter of dying*.

And where these went before, others follow.

And so the Christian dyingbed comes back again.

## XXXVI

# "Their Strength in the Time of Trouble"

## VICTORY THROUGH FAITH

THE invincible power of religion shows itself in the fact, that it goes beyond distress and death.

The waters of adversity cannot rise so high, but the real faith of God's child boldly strikes out the arms in them and knows how to keep the head above them.

Satan tried it with Job and asked leave of God Himself, to set Job as an example, whether it were not possible in the end altogether to extinguish and stamp out the spark of faith. But however much he plagued and taunted Job, robbed him of all he had and made a wretch of him sitting on the ash-heap, faith in Job in its flaming-up became impure, but *extinguished* it was not.

Whether Jeremiah indeed was cast into the miry pit and in the end stood alone over against all, so that his flesh rebelled against his soul, and he even said, that he wanted to give up the service of the Lord, yet he ended with finding his faith back again. "Lord, Thou art stronger than I, and hast prevailed" (Jer. 20, 7).

And as it was with the men of Scripture, so it was in all ages, and is so still. All white-washed and plastered religion falls from the wall, the moment heat scorches it or the stream rises up against it; but all real faith ever showed itself to be like hardest granite, from which scarcely with ax or pick-ax a single sliver can be knocked off.

O, it is sad history what the child of faith has struggled through not merely unintentionally from distress of soul, but what, worse yet, human wantonness or human error *intentionally* has done to the believer, to force him to deny his inmost conviction of soul; but yet in that somber history there is also *something* beautiful.

For in that blood-drenched history you see human cruelty and devilish malignity exhaust all its power, to invent the most cruel instruments of torture and to apply them in most excruciating ways, and yet in the end give up, because it availed nothing.

That the rack at length was abandoned and the torture-chamber became a museum of antiquities, is one of the most beautiful triumphs of religion. Not because she softened morals and has rendered public execution of justice less cruel, but because from this terrible struggle religion has come forth victorious, and the urge to torment at length gave up, because she saw, that she availed nothing against the faith.

Now, alas, this real religion, that is able in the end to triumph over every opposition, is not the common good of our human race.

When it came to it, almost always the majority stood on the side of the oppressors, and they who stood their ground were almost always and everywhere a very small minority.

True, there have been wonderful days in the struggle of the early Christian Church, as in the days of the Maccabees, heroic periods of faith in the valleys of the Waldenses and in the struggle of the Netherlands against Spain's superior power; days in which at length the power of faith prevailed and it seemed as though whole populations were moved by holier ardor.

But such conditions are an exception; and at least in our faithless time there is nowhere, in no single country anything left save a small kernel of the faithful, who still, if necessary, to witness to the name of the Lord, would die at the stake.

For there are still circles abroad in which the Christian faith is confessed, circles in which a certain measure of piety prevails, circles in which prayer is made and heaven is invoked. But even in these better circles so much gold glitters that is not gold, the plant of faith has struck so pitifully little root, and a single blast of the whirlwind would suffice to uproot the whole of this young park.

There is still much that is lovely. Praises are sung of Jesus, tributes of love are brought to His altar, to attain reconciliation for guilt of sin. Also an urge to entice others to Jesus. Not infrequently even a strong urge to shine in all sorts of works of charity and of virtuous practices. But of a faith that goeth out after God, unable to get along apart from the Eternal Being, and restlessly struggles to have one's refuge and one's invincible strength in God, with this half-faith you observe so little.


AND, of course, in the hour of trouble such a faith cannot maintain itself.

Religion is and ever remains a seeking, a loving, an affectionate honoring in the soul of the Eternal Being.

God the Lord, and He alone, to all real and genuine faith remains the center of the longings of our soul.

It all goes for His own sake. From Him genuine faith derives its real power. Nothing upon earth, nothing in heaven is comparable with Him, and no more ardent desire can be known, than in all anxiety and in all pain to be near unto the God of our life;—that, and that alone, is the glorious utterance of soul on the part of all true faith that is born of God.

From Him such faith is born, and therefore restlessly it draws toward Him.

Therefore it cries and pants after the living God, as a hart panteth after the water brooks.

To such an one God is his portion, his salvation, his eternal good.

And for the restless and violently moved heart there is no rest, until it can rest in God's everlasting love.

Of course, such faith then seeks the Mediator and with that Mediator the forgiveness in His blood; yet never otherwise than as means to get near unto God. Not to remain standing by the Mediator, but through Him by Whom we have access, to make our approach unto God.

It is for this reason, that true lovers of the Lord always reach out for the Psalms again; and that the dear friends, who are more concerned about a physician for the diseases of their soul, feel themselves more drawn to the hymns of Sankey.

For in those Psalms, you also find deliverance dealt with, there also the soul jubilates in the Mediator; but yet in those Psalms, amidst distress and death, it is and ever remains a calling out again after the living

God, an impetuous striving to reach His blessed fellowship.

No, the Psalmist is not one, who is anxiously bent upon obtaining for himself first of all a blessed little spot in heaven, whose chief concern is his own body's and soul's salvation, and who by a series of good works deems himself capable of balancing his account with heaven.

The Psalmist draws breath in spheres above this world. He peers through the veil of visible things. He therefore knows and seeks the Only One, the Eternal, Who hides Himself behind created things and exalts Himself above all things that are created.

Deep down in his soul he is awed and apprehended by the majesty of the Lord God.

Compared with Him, all that this world offers is esteemed as less than nothing; and therefore he knows, that no creaturely power, that presses upon him, can destroy him, because his God holds all that creaturely power in *His* hand, and against Him no creature *can* avail aught. With his God he leaps over a wall; with his God he pushes his way through an host.

He who has not come to this, and still lies down in the concern about the salvation of his soul, and is intent upon beautifying his own life with all sorts of virtue and good works, does not understand those deeper spiritual struggles and therefore cannot find those Psalms to be to his taste.

But he who on the pilgrim's journey of his faith has those first mile-posts back of him, and has passed over those first hills and gone through the valleys in the foreground, and now obtains a glimpse of the highland of God's holy mountains, to him religion begins to be a seeking after God Himself; and therefore those Psalms address him with so irresistible a power, that by the side of them every other song seems tame and dull.

To such an one dawns the light of his own soul's experience upon that glorious note of jubilation: "That God the Lord is a *strength* to His people *in the time of trouble*" (Ps. 37, 39).

No longer, as before, a God on Whom to call in times of suffering or accident, that He might avert it, or save them out of it, or heal them of their diseases.

To a certain extent unbelievers do so, too.

He who never prayed in other circumstances, frequently prays, when one dearly beloved, husband, wife or child, lies at death's door.

But for this very reason in such calling, without more, there is no religion yet. So we also call upon people. Similar help we also expect from our doctors.

No, "strength in the hour of trouble" means to say, that when the time of trouble comes, and we see, that God brings it upon us, and that there is no more escape from it, then so to abide in the midst of this distress and death, that a strength at work in us is evident, which in power excels the distress.

It is, in the hour of trial, to stand as the soldier on the field of battle. *Not* saying: Let us not fight! but, now that the battle is on, *bravely* fights, because he confides in his general, because the sacred cause for which the battle is on, beckons him, and because in his holy enthusiasm he loves the honor of his banner and the name of his general.

Under Napoleon overcame, he who without the strength, that went out from that name, would have been *defeated*.

And so, and in far higher sense, it behooves you, as God's child, so soon as the struggle begins, and you are personally involved in that struggle, to have *your strength* in the Name of the Lord, and of you it must be evident, whether the power of your God *to strengthen you,* is mightier than the influence of Satan and your own flesh to make you *succumb.*

Herein lay the mystery of martyrdom.

In that innermost experience of soul lay the secret of all triumph, which has ever been won by God's children.

That secret strength has become manifest, when scorn and shame choked the throat, when adversity and sorrow of soul almost made the waters go over the head, and also not least when one's own person was assaulted, in the hour of temptation to come to sin, or to apostacy in the hour of death.

For in death, of course, every creature forsakes you. Then every support which the world offered falls away from you. Then you are no longer even capable of holding on to your own body and to your own consciousness.

And then everything depends upon whether you can willingly cast yourself into the stream of death, trusting *alone* in the Lord your God.

## XXXVII

## "He Yielded Up the Ghost"

### YIELDING UP THE GHOST

THE world of the hidden life of our soul is so mysterious and baffling that, the older you become, the more you become aware, of that world of miracles which you carry about with you in your own inward life.

Numbers of questions here arise to which cleverest scholars cannot even begin to give an answer. They, who carry their studies outside of God's Word, lay indeed intricate problems before you regarding psychology, but the end always is, that they are unable to tell you, what the soul is, where she dwells, in what relation she stands with your body, what law she obeys, and how she operates.

In His Word God the Lord has spread so much light upon the life of our soul, as is needful for us, to live godly lives and to die in His peace; but answer to all sorts of questions of curiosity Holy Scripture does not give us.

The clearer and richer insight in that hidden world of our soul is here withheld from you, and comes only later on. When God the Lord had put Adam completed in Paradise, by his clearer sense Adam must have been more conscious of it than you; but yet to him also the background of the life of the soul must have remained mysterious. It does not belong to the "visible," but very positively to the "invisible" things, and over invisible things there ever hangs a veil.

It avails you therefore nothing, that with burning and passionate curiosity you try to penetrate this world full of mysteries. He who drives this too strongly, runs danger of becoming even insane. And for God's child the safest stand is, that, in humble faith you accept, what God has revealed to you, that you allow yourself to be led by that revealed knowledge, and rest therein with your pondering.

And the outcome has shown, that the life of the soul developed itself harmoniously and in beautiful simplicity, only when we did not try to look into what was withdrawn from our gaze, but quiet as the weaned child contented ourselves with what knowledge is revealed.

Especially one point then is fixed for you, namely this, that your soul and body are two, and, in that duality, are yet one. Different *in kind;* for your soul is something altogether different from your body, and your body is something altogether different from your soul; but yet also again *belonging together,* for without your soul your body becomes a corpse, and without your body your soul enters upon that separated and deprived state, which Paul, the holy apostle, prays against as a state of being "unclothed" and "naked."

He even speaks so strongly, that in 2 Cor. 5, 4 he does not hesitate to say: "We, who are still in the body, *groan,* being burdened, not that we would be unclothed, but clothed upon."

Of course this does not mean, that Paul *rebelled* against dying and did *not want* to die. Did he not equally have "a desire to be unbound and be with Christ?" It only means to say, that a temporal existence *as soul alone,* without body, is anti-natural for us; that therefore we always look to dying as to something that does violence to our nature; and being "burdened and groaning in ourselves," we long after our "unclothing" the sooner the better again to be clothed upon, that is to say, to obtain our body back again.

No Christian man therefore may say, that, so long as he but saves his soul, the body does not concern him.

He who says this does not honor God's holy ordinance.

For when God created man, he did not create *a soul,* but even created the body first, and breathed into that body the breath of lfe, and so man became a living soul.

Thus a soul is not a man. Man alone is he who has soul and body *both.* So death does violence to your existence-as-man. And then only shall the power of death be broken for you, when in the day of resurrection you obtain your glorified body back again, eternally to dwell in that body before the face of God.

BUT therefore your dying must also be such a dying, that you know what you do; and this the Scripture delineates in the ever-recurring expression, that he who dies *yields up the ghost.*

So at Jacob's dyingbed you see three operations of faith glisten.

First he sets his house in order and provides for his own. Then he lays himself down upon the bed, to die. And finally he dies.

Death to this patriarch is a pale stream of forgetful-

ness, into which he does not allow himself to be pushed,
into which he is not thrown, but into which he lets himself go down.

The spirit is not *taken from* him, but he *yields* up
the ghost.

And that with the old patriarch this was no over-
boldness nor imagination, Golgotha shows.

For there dies the Expectation of the fathers, and
also your Savior does not alone *give up* the ghost, but
acts therewith with so clear consciousness, that just
before He died He exclaimed with a loud voice: "Father,
into thine hands *I commend my spirit.*"

Even in our own mother-tongue that self-consciousness and self-activity on the part of him who goes into
death, is so beautifully expressed.

He who passes away, is not killed, but he doeth it
himself; he himself *dies.*

He *was* born, for this took place outside of himself; but in his departure he is no longer *passive.*

In dying *he dies himself.*

WHAT then in dying have you to do?

See it in Jesus, Who first commended His spirit
into His Father's hands, and then *gave up* the spirit.

By "spirit" here, which you are to give up, are you
to understand your *soul?*

Really not.

What in dying you give up is not your soul, but
your body. Also after dying you still have your soul;
but what after your dying, at least for a time, you have
*lost*, is your body.

Your soul does not leave you for a moment. Your soul goes with you, wherever you may go. From your soul you cannot even be separated. For even at times, when you lose your consciousness, and know nothing of your soul, your soul is ever present with you and you with your soul.

What you keep, you do not *give*, and cannot commend into the hands of another; and if you had to choose between soul and body, it would always yet be better sense to say, that he who dies gives up his body, rather than that he gives up his soul.

And yet, that you give up your body, is still something different from giving up the ghost.

And this also must be something different.

For it is easily understood, that he who in the midst of glowing youth and splendid health is suddenly overtaken by death, finds it a dreadful thing, to give up that sound, strong, flourishing body; while when you have become old, and all sorts of ailments and disease have come upon you, and the body creaks and grates in its structure, separation from that body is certainly not so hard, and many an one utters the humble prayer: "O, God, deliver me from this body, that so burdens and troubles me."

No, what in dying you have to do, is: *to give up the ghost,* and ghost here has no other meaning than "the breath of life."

Adam and spirit, both in the language of the Old and in the language of the New Testament, are frequently expressed by the same word. At one time it reads: "Thou takest away *their adem* (breath) and they die," and at another time that "the *spirit* returneth unto God Who gave it." And this occurs, not only with respect to man, but also to animals. For "that which befalleth the sons of men befalleth beasts; even one thing befalleth them: as the one dieth, so dieth the other; yea, they have all one breath" (Eccl. 3, 19).

Only when the "breath of life" goeth out from an animal, it never comes back; and when *you* breathe out that "breath of life" and give it over into God's hand, in the day of resurrection, God Almighty shall bring that "breath of life" back into you again.

Your spirit, your breath of life, which in dying you yield unto God, He preserves in His safe and holy hand, and in your resurrection that spirit comes back to you again.

In the meantime your soul is truly alive, and enjoys, after the nature of the soul, the blessedness of your Savior; but you miss that "breath of life," which here you had, simply because that "breath of life" is the wondrous secret, whereby God the Lord turned your body from a dead clod into an animated and living body.

So with Jesus that spirit, which He commended into the Father's hands, remained in that Father's hands, until that third morning, until He rose again, after God by giving back to Him that "breath of life" had quickened Him from the dead.

What thus also in your dying you have to do, is, that clearly conscious you have to acknowledge, that only by that breath or that spirit of life your soul stands related with your body; that now your soul must separate from that body; that this is possible only as that breath or that spirit of life is given back to God by you, by you is entrusted to His Father-hand; and that now you die in the assured hope and knowledge, that God Almighty shall once bring back again that "breath of life" in you, that after soul and body both again, and then eternally, you might live in His presence.

## XXXVIII

## "To Die Is Gain"

### DYING IS GAIN

THE art of piety, in which Paul excelled, consisted by no means in this, that he never thought of himself, but always of others.

Rather on the contrary Paul is every time and continuously busy with himself, and in almost every epistle you observe something personal of him.

No, but herein glistened the art of holy religion with Paul, that all his activity with his own person always came down again to the question, how in and with his own person he might make great the name of his Lord.

Thus no false mysticism, which loses itself in the effort, to cast himself away; but much more the sense of duty and calling, to make his own person, with all the talents, God had implanted therein, an instrument for God's glory.

This now is most strongly evident, when the holy apostle thinks of his own last end.

For when it comes to this, the involuntary sensation common to most people is: "Might that end in my case be deferred far, yea, yet very far, as far as possible."

And when serious sickness overtakes us, or when strength declines so perceptibly, that you scarcely dare to entertain any more hope, the second desire arises in us, that the Lord our God might make our dying as easy and calm as possible.

And when the sickness takes such a turn, that we can still think with sufficient clearness, to be busy with what comes *after* death, in that condition one utters mostly the third prayer, that after death one's soul may be safe with his Savior.

If now you hear Paul on the other hand, you must acknowledge yourself, that this man of God had made further advances.

Of that cleaving to life there was no more mention with him. His desire rather was to be unbound and to be with Christ.

Of easy and calm dying he had no thought. He well knew, that he was to die on the scaffold, and therefore he exclaimed: "As a drink-offering I am to be offered."

And about his salvation he was not in the leastwise troubled, for with full assurance of faith he knew, "That there was laid up for him a crown of righteousness" (II Tim. 4, 8).

No, all he was concerned about was, "Whether *Christ would be magnified, also by his death*" (Phil. 1, 20).

Now you yourself grant, that only this is the real; and that in such a noble word the art of piety celebrates a rare triumph.

And when you ask, wherein lay the secret of this art, he himself discovers this to you, when immediately he adds: *"For to me to die is gain"* (Phil. 1, 21).

As for himself, he would not hesitate one moment. So far as he was concerned, he would rather die to-day than to-morrow. And that he is ready to continue the pilgrim-journey yet farther, is merely because, he does not yet clearly know and perceive, whereby he shall magnify yet more the name of Christ, by continuing his struggle upon earth, or by just dying now.

Thus all his strength consisted in this, that he lived in the full assurance of faith.

No anxiousness and no being tossed about. No cleaving to and no hankering after. No halfway consent and yet again not.

There is never strength in this. This wearies and murders the soul. This is holding faith under, instead of letting it healthfully flourish.

And Ministry of the Word, that degrades itself in feeding and coddling these endless troubles and uncertainties of faith, stands therefore guilty before God; for so all spiritual elasticity in God's child and in God's church is broken.

What the Ministry of the Word must do is to steady feeble knees and lift up hands that hang down, and from the root itself of faith let the full, rich, glad assurance of faith spring up as the fragrant flower.

He who does not know and confesses: "I have been apprehended of my God, because chosen: and, when I die, now or ten years hence, the golden harp and palm-branch await me!" has really no count among the satellites and holy picked troops of the Lord.

Satan, who is always on the alert, to move you this way and that as a reed; but Christ's church must establish you in fixedness.

So Paul, so our fathers understood it, and therefore

they were so disciplined in the holy art *of religion,* which is nothing else than the art *of faith*.

*For me to die is gain*.

Not *perhaps;* possibly; if at least the Lord grants me grace.

No, but positively; as something that stands wall-sure and speaks of itself.

Not only does he not *lose* by dying, but he *gains* thereby. His lot and condition shall improve thereby. And that nevertheless he is ready to go on living, is only because it must never be the question, whether *he* gains, but how there may be greatest gains for Christ's name.

*For me to die is gain*. Does this mean to say, that Paul represented dying to himself as so easy a matter, and that he had no knowledge of the bitterness of death?

But we already reminded you, how he saw ahead of him no other dying than on the scaffold, by the violence of human hands; and as regards death, who else than Paul called him: *the last enemy?*

No, the man who jubilated: *"For me to die is gain,"* was by no means a sentimental person, who set store by it, that after his death it would be reported to his friends, that Paul had fallen asleep, O, so *easily* and *calmly*.

Better than any one this wondrous man of Tarsus knew, that even after dying there still follows the state of deprivation; that, as he expresses it, we shall then be "unclothed"; shall miss our body and world of our life; and that this must last until the time of the consummation of the ages, and Christ returns, and He makes us rise again in our glorified body, only after that in the realm of glory to reign with Him as kings.

Illusions this hero of faith knew none.

Clearly and soberly he realized, what *at* dying, *in* dying and *after* dying would happen with him.

And still he gloried: *"For me to die is gain,"* because his life on earth was so full of struggle and anxiety; because trouble and vexation every time again overwhelmed his heart; and above all because then he would be delivered from the body of this death, to be eternally with his Jesus.

ALSO for you, when your sick-room becomes your prison and your end draws near, it is thus necessary, that clearly and soberly you picture to yourself, what, when the last moment comes, is to happen with you; what shall happen with you in the dying itself; and where and how you will find yourself, when your soul has been torn asunder from your body.

In that dying there always remains a bitter cup to be drunk, for it is in opposition to our nature. And as a child of God it does not behoove you, to talk this away, to put it away from you, or to cover it over with flowers. With that sacred courage, which can shine out equally in the heart of man and woman, you must look death in the face, but death as one who has been *overcome* of your Lord and Savior.

And rest, peace for your inner sense in that face of death can only be yours, when you are sure, that also upon this winter there follows a spring; and know for yourself and of yourself, that that death shall no more be for you a wage for your sin, but the entrance upon *life eternal.*

Still to be spared in life can and may be the prayer of your heart; provided it be not for yourself; for that always implies, that you still count the termination of your life here as *loss,* and in the *continuance of life* here still see gain. A token, that you do not know the struggle and the shame for Jesus' sake, and the "being forever with the Lord" you esteem indeed very highly, but ever yet esteem it *inferior* to the happiness which you now enjoy.

And now I do not say, that every child of God always therefore stands right in this matter. Nature asserts itself strongly. And sometimes the glory of the stars on high has gone in hiding behind heavy clouds. But in moments of clear limpid faith the soul must be brought to terms, and dying must never menace you as *loss,* but always glisten before you as *gain.*

ONLY two things can dying make you pray for. First, for what Paul says: "To abide in the flesh is more needful for you" (Phil. 1, 24); and secondly, for what he assures us: not to know as yet whether he can magnify Jesus' name more by still continuing in life, or by dying already now.

A high, very high standpoint, to be sure, and yet not *too* high, but the common and normal standpoint of the child of God.

Yet this also shows in a dreadful way, how deeply God's people have more and more sunken away from the high standpoint of faith; for in all honesty, in what sick-room, or on what dyingbed do you now hear of such deliberations? More still, how many are the dying-beds, of which you can say, that the name of the Lord is magnified by them?

Truly no complaint is made of this, arrogantly to look down upon others, for where is the man, who can put this question, without thereby including himself?

This comes of it, that, yielding to the spirit of the age, Death is passed by in silence, and in preaching also the great question of dying has been consigned to the background.

And forsofar this constant reference to death in times past was done mostly in church to make women weep, or also egotistically to be more certain after death of one's own safety, there was a sobriety in this that deserves praise.

But because *ill-advised* preaching about dying must be disapproved, *good* preaching about Death may therefore not be neglected.

Every time again the Ministry of the Word must bring us to the gates of Death; not in one's own behalf nor for self-glorification, but always again with the prayer on one's lips, that all God's people, not only the aged, but also young men and maidens, yea, even our very children, may *also in their dying magnify the name of Christ*.

## XXXIX

## *"The End of That Man Is Peace"*

### THE END OF THAT MAN WAS PEACE

PEACE is something divinely glorious; for "peace" does not merely mean, that you are *outside* of trouble and struggle, but altogether differently, that an enemy stands or stood over against you, that that enemy lives, and that danger threatened you from all sides, and that it was evident, that you had to go under, and that now, a higher power has stepped in between, and that your enemy was either rendered powerless or has become a friend to you; and that now anxiety is lifted from your soul and the struggle is ended, and danger gone; and that in place of mortal anxiety and struggle and distress of soul there entered in an, O, so soul-uplifting and soul-refreshing feeling of rest and of peace.

He who can say: I have peace! is not the coward who ran away from the fray or held himself aloof from the battle. No, peace is the wage of the victor, the prize of bravery and of perseverance wherewith the battle was fought. Peace, which means to him who almost sank away and perished, particularly this one thing: that God the Lord decided the matter in his behalf, and *granted* him peace.

"Peace on earth!" this God's angels did not sing in Paradise, when the conflict had not yet broken out, but "Peace on earth!" this sang God's heavenly hosts at the well of Bethlehem, when He was about to be born, Whose coming to this earth was not to bring peace, but the sword.

And when the Son of God parted from His disciples and said to them: "Peace I leave with you, my peace I give unto you!" it truly was not to open a future to them, in which they were to walk a path of roses, neither for Himself already to enter upon glory; for He went to Gethsemane and every one of His apostles went toward the martyrdeath; and therefore the Lord added so emphatically: "*Not* as the world giveth, give I unto you!"

And therefore, if we will listen to God's holy Word, "peace" has nothing, absolutely nothing in common with the sweetly holding oneself apart from the strife, which may not even be called "life," let alone "peace." "Peace" is the divine exaltation of soul on the part of him, who has overcome. "Peace" is to live anew from the blossom of strength that was developed in the mortal strife. "Peace" is *no more* to fight, but to be above the battle, and now to feel coming down into, to feel shining out in the heart, the sweet, the beauty and the desirable of full-blessed harmony.

STAND for such peace among men!

Two sorts of things among men can disturb your peace, the peace of your soul; for strife can come, when some one with whom you have to do, will not go out of the way for you; but there also can come strife, because he will not go out the way for God's truth.

With that first sort of strife the choice of what you have to do is not difficult. Then indeed, yourself to go out of the way, is *always* your duty. It is as well the duty of the other, so that it is most glorious, when together by grace coming to recognize this, at a given moment both vie to give in, and the struggle no more is as to who may win, but as to who may lose. But even when the other does not listen to that admonition, for you this makes no difference. You may never seek to save your soul, for every time you do this, you lose her. Always be the least. Seventy times seven forgive. The Shepherd of our souls knows no exception.

But it is altogether different, when the battle does not center around you, but around God's truth, for then you may not give in. Not do, as those cowards do, who, to keep peace, say nothing of anything, and then, in their cowardice imagine, that the beatitude of the peaceable is applicable to themselves. No, for God's sake and right and Word and truth the battle must ever be on. Not only, not mostly even by abstract advocacy of the same, but above all and then mostly, when, in daily intercourse with people, in education, in dealing with matters of calling, a grain of the gold of God's right and truth might be darkened, and we see it, O, then we may not keep silent, but the fight must be fought, and then, alas, yes, the peace, the peace especially among those who are nearest related or nearest united, is gone.

O, then fight the fight of God purely; fight it uprightly; never call anything a fight for the Lord's sake, when in some hidden corner of your heart it is yet and really again for the sake of your own *self*.

Above all fight in prayer, and though the battle lasts long, will, desire, accept never any other peace than that, by which your brother is won and the cause of God triumphs.


STAND for this peace with yourself.

Every heart, that is alive, must begin with being in altercation with itself.

There truly is difference of character, and with one the wavebeat of the troubled breast goes higher than with the other, but yet, a stagnant morass is the human heart of him alone, that is lost, and with every child of God there is always the wind that beats down from above, the breath of the Spirit, to beat upward the waters of his soul, and that breath of the Spirit gives him no rest.

While young one feels this best, be it as yet not sharpest. He who is still young, finds it natural, that he has not yet found peace. But, and see here for the most part the mistake of the youthful mind, one then imagines, that after a struggle of say seven long years that battle shall be ended and the ideal of perfect peace shall have been reached.

And that then ends in disappointment. For he who watches his soul sharply finds, that he goes rather backward than forward. Not really, but because his life expands itself and temptation multiplies. And then most people effect a compromise. Weary of struggling they seek to come to some understanding with themselves. They let their once so glorious ideal lower; they now find, that something must be conceded to the world; and so they extinguish their fires, and lie quietly at anchor.

And this then is said to be at peace with oneself.

O, blessed is he, who never, not for one single moment, was charmed in behalf of his own soul, by so false a peace.

PSALMNODY therefore also knows another note.

Almost always the battle-song: "Work while it is day, for the night cometh wherein no man can work," and only at the last mile-post comes the soul-satisfying refreshment of the: "God crowns *the end* of His servants with peace."

Not that already in the midst of life a part of peace should not descend into the soul of a child of God.

Of course, the first, fierce, wild battle, whether he will stand for Satan or for God, no, that does not go on till our dying. That is decided long in advance. And after anxious distress of soul there comes insofar peace indeed, peace already now, peace already here on earth, that our soul stands fixed and certain, and also knows, that Satan himself can never here or yonder snatch her more out of the hand of the Father.

More still, in addition to this, parts of that peace the Lord sometimes gives His redeemed to taste, when there are edges to their character, and sinful tendencies in their soul, and battles rage around about them, whereby and wherein for long time they were vanquished, and however much in the need and death of their soul they labored, they could not come, where they well knew they ought to be. For, yea, also in such struggles already here on earth the Lord gives victory, and after the triumph peace, that the soul may rejoice: "I have fought the good fight, I have finished my course, henceforth the crown is laid up for me!"

But *the* peace, the absolute, the full-blessed peace, no, that only comes at the end. Not when one becomes aged, and not even yet when one comes to die, but only *when* one dies, and if then the end may be peace.

For this is sure: So long as we are in this body of death and dwell in this world of sin, it is not yet the perfect deliverance and not yet the heavenly tenderness. Then the evil *self* may slumber, without tossing much about, but it is ever yet alive, and *the* peace, O, when that shall come upon you, nothing, nothing more must be wanting from the eternal peace. O, then it must lie so sacredly even and pure as the level between you and that glorious, holy, thrice holy God.

Therefore that highest, that richest, that *full* peace, which comes at the end, is then also no wage, but a crown.

Grace grants it unto us.

Grants it sometimes to a young child, to withhold it from an old man.

But yet, however sovereign God's grace may be, with that peace He does not crown "sinners" in the end.

They shall perish, but the anointed of the Lord shall remain standing.

And then the battle is ended, and ended the trouble, and the insinking, and the blush of shame.

And then comes the peace.

The peace of the Eternal to reign eternally.

O, in that anxious hour, brothers, be this the blessed portion of us all.

## *"To-day with Me in Paradise"*

### IS HE SAVED?

ESPECIALLY when death tries to climb in through the windows of our home, and fear takes hold of us, that our sick is going to die, we feel sometimes so somber-seriously the question cast into our soul: *Shall he be saved?*

There are those, praise the Lord, whom we see pass away from our environment, without that anxious question disquieting us for one moment. Brothers and sisters, of whose person, from whose word and by whose whole appearance we received so strong an impression of an *Abba Father,* that it could not be strange, that their departure *must* have been an entrance into the blessedness.

Truly, our human judgment is always fallible, and with the best of us our spiritual insight can deceive itself; but, provided our judgment does not rest upon weak impressions, but upon serious investigation, we need not detain ourselves with it. Not we are seated on the tribunal, God is judge; and standing at the dyingbed of our loved ones, it is already so glorious, if we have no anxiety of soul regarding their eternal salvation; when, weeping at their grave, we feel no concern about their blessedness of soul cutting in the deeply-moved heart.

Be not anxious therefore nor melancholy, and when from your association in earlier and healthier days you received a happy impression, that the features of childship shone through brightly, do not then burden your soul with sombernesses, which have no ground, but rather thank your God, that He included your sick in the bundle of the living.

Not the spiritual *condition* under depressing pain decides; it depends alone upon the spiritual *state*.

And though in distress and death's extremity there is still much struggle, yea, though everything seems to be gone, never may the lot for eternity be measured off thereby.

For, surely, there is something, O, so glorious, when there may be a rich, a witnessing, a jubilant, an almost prophetical dyingbed.

But also such a triumphant and comforting dyingbed is pure grace, and also in the imparting of this grace the God of all compassion remains free.

MAKING up on the dyingbed what in days of strength and prosperity was so recklessly neglected, almost *never succeeds*.

Appearance here deceives.

Indeed there are not a few, who in the shadows of death break through into freedom, into largeness of space and to spiritual melting; but in most instances this touches only *faith-assurance*.

They had long since exchanged play for seriousness. Thirst after righteousness burned, O, so long already upon their lips. Without the Savior they would not do. Only, they remained uncertain about appropriation, and they lacked the joy of personal faith. They sought assurance along a way, which does not lead thereto, and they overlooked the fact, that assurance belongs to the nature itself of faith, and therefore germinates alone from faith itself in the broken heart.

If one is once carried along in these streams of doubts and anxieties, and lives in an environment, which encourages these tossings, and one hears preaching, that gives no direction regarding it, yea, then with these children of God it remains to their latest days anxious questioning, and not infrequently it is only shortly before their dying that full light breaks through in their soul.

Not as though only at that late moment the first grace was spent on them. That grace operated already long years.

But only now the scales fall from the eyes and they *see* the light.


For the rest on the other hand, there prevails at all too many dyingbeds a dull, spiritless tone, and upon, O, so many a grave there stands a soul-gripping interrogation-mark.

What was this dying? An entrance upon eternal life, or a forever sinking away into the bands of hell and death?

This renders it indeed so intelligible, especially when the doctor says that there is no more hope, that so often a last effort is made, to call the dying to the Savior.

And this is needful. And provided it takes place from the urge of holy love, and not from hard haughtiness, this is always praiseworthy.

Sometimes it also bore fruit.

Only, such admonition to the dying so frequently bore the character of making up of neglect.

A mother, who in days of health had let her husband, her child spiritually grow in the wild; who even in the first days of sickness, when as yet there was no danger, had merely engaged in small talk; and now, in the extreme moment, sobered by the approaching death-struggle, suddenly reminds herself, that also her husband, her child has a soul to lose forever, and now deems to be able by a pressing word to make up what was left undone.

And in most cases this avails nothing.

Because she does not understand the art of it; because the poor sufferer is already too far gone and too confused; and also because God has promised no blessing upon such doings.

But from such effort of despair there truly goes out a cry from the conscience to all living: Even now, in the acceptable time, now in the day of grace, consider for yourself, and consider for your loved ones, what pertains to your eternal peace.

AND do you ask, whether, when one of our dear ones passed away, without giving us before dying any sign of spiritual life, we should pass judgment, that he who died is lost—then the answer runs: *You are not to judge. He Who judges the living and the dead, is the Lord.*

Thus you should not say: "He may indeed be saved." Where no ground was evident, you have no ground. And at least in this holy matter of such dreadful seriousness you shall not lie.

If nothing of childship in the dead was discovered by you, you miss every right, to say, that God will yet be gracious unto him.

Neither are you permitted to pray for the deceased any more, that God will yet be gracious unto him; for though the word of the Preacher "as the tree falleth, so shall it lie" has a somewhat different sense, yet the thought expressed therein by God's people, is altogether true.

On this side of the grave there must be life in the soul and light in the eye of the soul, or else it does not come.

On the other side of the grave there is no more place for conversion.

Only think of the rich man in the parable.

"Between us and you there is a great gulf fixed, so that they which would pass from hence to you cannot" (S. Luke 16, 26).

BUT, and this needs to be emphasized, you should just as little say: *"He is lost,"* for also that you do not know.

When Calvin was told of the fanatic assassin, who had stabbed the Duke de Guise, he said: "No one knows whether in his deathcry God has not shown mercy to the duke."

God's absolute power you shall not limit.

To infuse grace unto life is the work of an indivisible moment, and you can never say, what it may please God, even yet in such a latest moment, even yet in the last gasp to do to the dying.

You may not say, that it is so. You miss even every

ground of hope, on which to rest. But the possibility remains, and already this stops despair.

With all the children of God dying is a *dying away of sin;* and who observes anything of it, that in dying God brings to effect this cutting off of all sin and this perfecting of sanctification?

Of God's hidden working in the soul we take notice later on, when the fruit of it becomes evident; but when the Holy Spirit finishes the internal hidden work, is a secret to us.

Thus you are to pass no judgment. Not to glory in a salvation, of which you have no knowledge. Not to soothe yourself with general talk without seriousness. Neither yet to make mention of a hope, for which you have no ground.

You have to leave it with God, and gratefully to acknowledge the possibility, that grace *can* still have been quickened.

THE "This day shalt thou be with me in Paradise" also came so altogether unexpectedly.

Jesus' disciples have taken to flight. Judas has betrayed Him. Peter has denied Him. Only John is seen at the cross. Only a few women persevere in their love. And while all these children of God shudder and tremble and sin, it is that murderer on the cross, to whom Jesus unlocks the gate of Paradise.

So has Jesus in dying on the shamewood thought of our dying ones, and by that striking word to the crossling in his death agonies, has restored to innumerable thousands of souls, who in their dying despaired, yet in that dying itself courage and the hope of salvation.

O, in dying even best piety falls away, and so naked and in her shame does our soul come to stand before her God. The distance between the murderer and a dear child of God like John dwindles so greatly in the hour of death.

It is then *purely* grace. Nothing indeed save a "Lord Jesus, receive my soul!"

And therefore in days of somber seriousness look not upon your dying, look not upon your dead, gaze not upon his tombstone, but gaze solely upon the grace of your Lord, so absolutely powerful, so divinely compassionate and so rich.

## XLI

## *"As a Flower of the Field"*

### A FLOWER OF THE FIELD

Our warm sympathy for the world of flowers is no invention of our own heart. God Himself created those flowers for us, and us so, that we enjoy those flowers, feel relation to those flowers, and also can understand *the language of those flowers.*

For, those flowers address us with a speech, which God has laid in them, and in beautiful forms, luxurious fragrance, in tints that enchant the eye, interpret to us, children of men, the course of our own lot in life.

Scripture therefore never wearies, ever and again to point us to that world of flowers. You know what it relates of the lily among the thorns, and of the rose of Sharon. From the sermon on the mount you know Jesus' moving reference to the lilies of the field, more beautifully clothed by God, than in all his glory Solomon was ever clothed. And you know no less, how Scripture every time again points you to the grass and to the "flowers of the field," to remind you of the transitoriness of your human existence.

Especially in the East, where it pleased God to have the Scripture originate, the fieldflower is so incredibly short-lived and evanescent. With the warm climate it springs up as by a wondergrowth quickly in the midst of blades of grass. At once you see a field, that yesterday was green with grass alone, gayly adorned with thousands of little flowers, which opened their yellow and blue and red cups. But just as quickly all that beauty can be gone again. When but for half a day the scorching wind of the desert has passed over it, all the grass lies withered, and amidst that withered grass those thousands of faded fieldflowerets are scarcely any more findable.

And with an eye to this the Psalmist says so beautifully, that *your* life also is not so unlike to the life of that fieldflower in the grass.

"As for man, his days are as grass, as a flower of the field, so he flourisheth; but just so soon as the wind has passed over it, it is gone, and the place thereof knoweth it no more" (Ps. 103, 15).

Especially with the ever continuous dying of so many little darlings that fieldflower addresses you so touchingly, and never better than at the grave of those little ones do you understand that quiet disappearing, as the trackless snatching away of the fieldflower in the grass.

Mature persons in their dying impress us differently. They had taken more root. Long years they had summered and wintered by and with us. Their person and character had assumed more fixed forms. They occupied a broader place. And when finally they left us, we received more the impression of a trunk that was felled, than of a fieldflower, that broke on its stem and at once was gone.

But when God the Lord calls away little children, to come unto Him, is not then that fieldflower, which blossomed so briefly and then so silently disappeared, the touching accurate expression of what you observed?

In that little, young life there was so little trunk as yet, it was still all *flower*. No flower yet on a high stem, but a fieldflower hidden in the grass and but just lifting up its colorful little head above that grass. And now came the wind from the desert, the wind, that carried in itself the breath of death. And under that touch it succumbed. The litle head bent itself; the colors paled, the unfixed forms melted. And so it disappeared; to leave behind nothing but a hovering image, and round about it memories at play. Memories sacred only in a narrower circle, of which the world has no knowledge, because so young a child is not able to capture a place for itself in that world.

So it was a coming, to go; an appearing, to disappear. And so they die away by hundreds and thousands, those little darlings, known of God, but passed by unnoticed of men.

Fieldflowerets, which God had sown, and which God's angels plucked away again.

They were not for here.

God had appointed them as ornaments for His holy temple.

That dying of these little ones is therefore so rich in significance; and you miss so much, when you pass lightly over their mysterious disappearing.

When a great man passes away, there is always so much to be said *about that great man*, that there is almost no notice taken of God's doing; but at the deathbed and at the grave of an infant God's doing is so largely the one and all that counts.

That little infant had scarcely yet reason for existence, otherwise than in what God intended to do with him; and of that plan of God with such a child you scarcely knew anything, and even now you know so little. It was as a book of which you read the first ten pages; and then it was taken out of your hands. All the rest of it remains to you always a deep hiddenness.

Neither have you any token, with such an infant, by which to estimate his piety, from which piety to form any idea of his part in God's grace, and so to place your hope on what was before your eyes. For also in the life of the soul everything was here equally enigmatical. All that was done in and to that hidden life of the soul, was done by God.

Because of his years that infant was still so altogether passive, and a work of grace could be there solely from the side of God.

A single ray of higher light might at times have broken through. A tender childlike word may have sweet echoes in the memory. But yet, all that had too little substance to it, for you to build upon. What with such an infant you build upon, is only what God spake of this little one; what addresses you with all blessing and comfort, is His holy and glorious *promise;* what as an event of the past pours rest into the soul, is his holy Baptism.

For in that Baptism He told you, that no child can die so young, but that it can have been operated upon by Him with grace.

That you, who are older in years, have read a little more and heard and known, makes no difference.

God's work of grace is not dependent upon your intellectual development; and the fieldfloweret, that scarcely unfolded to wither again, was as well bedewed by the dew of heaven as the cedar and the palm tree, which still resist the storms.

A CHILD of God therefore tarries with his ponderings so willingly at the dying of the little darlings, because especially at their dying and at their grave God the Lord is so great.

In His doing with these little ones there is such speechless majesty.

We *thought* we knew them, but understood almost nothing as yet of them, while God saw through and knew all the being of the little ones, knowing all the germs, which for an eternal growth were increated by Himself in their soul.

Just think that an Abraham or an Isaiah, a Paul or a John had died as little lambs, the world would never have imagined from far, what had died away in them. But God would have seen it, and would have been on guard, that with their departure nothing that had aught of eternal worth would be lost.

And therefore it is so offensively foolish of us, to deem, that only they, who have become important personages here on earth, shall also be great in heaven, and as though these millions of little ones, who died young, shall scarcely be of any count.

Why should not God have among these little ones His choice spirits, His chosen instruments?

With us they were conceived and born in sin; of course. They were dead as we, and can have no life except through regeneration, no atonement save in Christ's blood.

But how great is their advantage, that with them the *dying unto sin* took already place so early, and that that hard, cruel development of bosomsin, which often weighs so heavily upon God's children, was almost altogether spared them!

How slow is our development in the knowledge of God, while for them in death suddenly and at once the full light dawned.

*Why* God calls away one-half of the children of men so early, we know not. *What* the reason is, that He brings one-half of His elect to blessedness so altogether differently from the other half, that remains behind on earth, is a question, that forces itself upon us every time again, but which God does not answer.

He, the Lord, remains the all-powerful, the Sovereign God, Who doeth not alone with us, but also with our children according to His good pleasure.

But however different our lot may be from theirs, there is connection between their soul's existence and the life of our own soul.

Not with every child that dies young is there mention of blessedness. Without the deep root of election no blessedness can flower, as little with us as with our baptized children. And so it is *believing parents* only, of whom it is said, that they must not doubt the blessedness of their children, whom God calls away early from this life.

No sentiment, no emotional play of feeling, *faith alone* remains here also the starting point.

He who *believes*, that is to say, he who by a propelling power, that springs from the root of the life of his soul, practices personal fellowship with the Eternal Being, through the Mediator, can in this faith also not let go of his young deceased child, but in his God finds powers, and with his God ways, and in His Word light, and by His Spirit blessed comfort, at the grave also of what was his own flesh and bone, to glory in the face of death, and, with his seed hidden in Jesus, to rest in the majesty of his God.

## XLII

# "He Bindeth Up Their Wounds"

### THE LORD BINDETH UP YOUR WOUNDS

"Sing unto the Lord with thanksgiving; sing praise upon the harp unto our God," (147, 7) for, so the Holy Ghost bears witness through the Psalmist, *"for our Lord is great."*

And what are the four things, in which that greatness of our God shines out most strongly?

First therein, that He builds up Jerusalem. That is and always remains His highest work of art. Then His majesty is so mightily manifest, that He telleth the number of the stars and knoweth them all by name. In the third place His greatness speaks in His battle against the godless and in the support which He offers His faithful people. But in the fourth place also our God is therein so worshipfully great, *"That He healeth the broken in heart, and bindeth up their wounds"* (147, 3).

Our God wills *always* to be thanked and praised.

Not only in moments of rich gladness; but thanked and praised also by those lips, which He himself has closed up in sorrow, and from that heart, which He himself deeply wounds.

Even then praise is comely, because that selfsame God, Who wounds, is also then rich in love.

Then bitter grief first forces from the troubled heart pitiful lamentations and complaints; but in that complaining there is always something sinful.

God may *never* be complained against; He must *always* be magnified and praised.

Praised and thanked in such a way, that also in your deepest grief you feel that you *love* your God, because you experience how also in that distress of heart *He loves you first.*

Hence no reasonings; no speaking to yourself with words; but an observing how tenderly God loves you in your griefs, and therefore kiss the hand, not that *strikes*—that you cannot do—but that *struck*, and now so divinely compassionately binds you up in your sorrow.

Not as though some one else inflicted the blow, and that now God comes to bind you up. That would occasion endless restlessness, and Scripture directly opposes the suggestion. It reads so clearly: "The Lord grieves and He binds up. The Lord wounds, and His hands heal." That it is the Lord, *Who kills*, the Holy Ghost reiterates so emphatically, that we might be instructed regarding it, when one dies away from the circle of our domestic wealth.

He who dares not face this, and does not see clearly into this, cannot taste the sweet, in his distresses of soul to be bound up by his God.

Something of this, by way of comparison, the child of a physician can experience on earth, when, *because it was necessary*, that child was so painfully operated on by his own father. But now the operation is over. The knife, to which blood cleaves, is laid aside. And now comes that selfsame father, no more with knife but with lint and balsam in hands, and with a tear in the eye and with tender care, that excels itself, he binds up the deep wound, which with his own hand, *because it was necessary*, he inflicted in the flesh of his child.

True, the figure is weak. To whom indeed would you liken God? But, however weak, it tells you something of what God does to you.

He took action; He cut in deep; *because it was necessary*. He not only wounded, but wounded you through and through. Anything less deep, the wound would have been purposeless, useless pain. To the fineness of a hair your Father in the heavens knew, how deep the incision had to be cut into your soul.

But see, no sooner is the painful operation ended, but the sacred lint and the divine balsam are already at hand; and that same divine hand, which so deeply wounded you, now turns itself to you in divine compassion, and He Himself binds up your wounds.

### He Himself

Not as though human pity also would not operate soothingly upon the wound of your heart. Every expression of sympathy on the part of a fellow-man is refreshing. And when God gives you a brother, who understands you; who lives equally deeply as you yourself live; or also one, who suffered as you suffered, and with the experience of his own heart comes to your heart, that human comforting can already affect you soothingly and beneficently.

Provided, and this belongs to it, you see and recognize, that it is God, Who unlocked that brotherheart to you, poured out tenderness in it for you, and animated it with a word, which He had intended for you.

Yea, really it should be said, that such a human comforting only operates efficaciously upon you, when he who comforts you does not do it for his own sake, but lets himself be used of his God, to comfort you, and to His glory.

So viewed, it is already in that human comforting your God, Who comes to your aid, and appointed this for you.

But He does not leave it with this.

He is not a God afar off, Who leaves this soothing work of comforting in the hands of others, but He comes Himself.

O, when more than in such moments was your God ever near by; in your hidden dwelling; entering into your heart; and when ever more strongly than in such a struggle have you felt the Holy Ghost operating within you, praying with you and praying for you with groanings unutterable?

*He binds up their wounds.*

So the Word testifies, and so age after age it has been experienced by God's saints.

For in such days of bitter anxiety God's saints are so highly privileged.

Not as though that merciful Father, Who makes His sun to shine on the evil and the good, should not also come to those other children for their help with His grace; only they take no notice of it. They do not taste the sweet and blessedness of the same. In the days of their grief and of their mourning they are so poor.

But God's child is so rich.

Then he who believes, lies down, and his wound, the wound of his heart, bleeds so badly. It causes so great inward pain. Faith makes sensitiveness; and insofar suffering is made heavier by faith. Also God's child then observes his own powerlessness. Everything storms in upon him. Conscience drives so strongly from within. His whole being is put to grief. But, and this is so glorious, in the midst of that crying sorrow of heart he also observes, that his God has dealings with him.

And when his God then comes to him, and in the Father-eye of his God he reads that deep, divine expression of unspeakable compassion, then something draws through his soul, that lifts up his entire being in grace, and he sees, he perceives, how much his God loves him; and to realize this, is comfort; *that* soothes the pain.

AND yet, even with this the Lord does not leave it.

In such moments He not merely looks upon you with the eye of His divine compassion in so comforting a way, but He also comes with His almighty hand to bind up your wounds.

He, Who sees the wound not only from outside, but looks into it down to the root of the life of your soul; yea, Who fathoms it more deeply than you fathom it yourself; and, so to speak, knows more accurately than you know yourself, what of loss, of sorrow and of anguish of soul, also with respect to your future there hides in that wound of your heart.

And then He proceeds to bind up that wound.

Then He relaxes the nervous tension, and grants you grace, that you can weep, and that yet again in your tears you can control yourself.

Then in the hiddenness of your being He fortifies your heart, and stops that bleeding, and arrests that outpouring of cutting pain.

Then He applies His holy balsam, that it aches no more so badly, and covers your wound, that sensitiveness may not outdo your strength.

Yea, then He enswathes and enwraps your soul with gentle operations of grace, till at length the wound in its painful working is tempered.

And as then imperceptibly the divine bandage has been applied, He does not go away, but remains with you, and hands you the cup of the elixer of life, and stimulates again the glorious working of your faith.

He then brings you His Jesus richly and gloriously before the soul. Not to divert you, but to teach you, how in the work of your Savior such conditions were taken into account.

That deep, divine cross of Golgotha, in which sinks away the whole world of your heart, and from which reconciled and enriched it always comes up again.

O, your God is so great; the Lord is so lovely. Yea, truly in such days also praise is comely.

And as the wound of your heart has been bound up of your God and you lie down under the shadow of His tender Father care, no, then it is no more at a cost, and you no longer have to do violence to yourself; but then it goes with such affectionate tenderness and so heartily, that you thank God for His tender compassion; and if then there are those who suffer with you, then indeed, it becomes a singing by turns with thanksgiving; for then *in* and *by* your grief God has enriched you.

## XLIII

## *"Moved with Compassion"*

### OUR TEARS

ALSO our Savior has known moments time and again, in which strong *emotions* threatened to overmaster Him.

We constantly read, that at the sight of our human misery He was inwardly *moved* and *stirred*. Sometimes even the Evangelists add, that He was *very greatly* moved and *strongly* stirred; moved with *compassion*; moved with *mercy*; deeply moved *in spirit*, as at Lazarus' grave, or deeply affected *in spirit*, as at the announcement of the treason; until at length with Him also emotion became too overpowering to inwardly smother it, and also gave Jesus an outlet in the tear, that trickled down His cheek.

Also Jesus has *wept*. Wept at Lazarus' grave; wept over Jerusalem's unwillingness to convert herself to her God. And not least in that weeping did it become evident, how violently He could inwardly be shocked and moved.

Yea, deepest of all Jesus was inwardly assaulted, altogether amazed and appalled, when in Gethsemane He underwent satanic temptation and He bent Himself down under the burden of our guilt and our sin, until anxious sweat broke out from Him and God's angel had to support Him.

Also that was a violent, inward emotion affecting His whole being, of which in the anxiety of terror He

Himself complained to His disciples: *"My soul is* exceeding sorrowful unto death" (S. Mark 14, 34).

Jesus' example therefore shows, how such emotions of our heart have their right of human existence; that impassiveness is no virtue; that blunting of our feeling is no fruit of faith; and that to remain stolid in most striking moments of our life, betrays a condition of mind and heart, which has its place with stoical philosophers, but is not at home with children of God.

The familiar story, that after the fall an angel of God brought man a tear from heaven as a means of divine comforting, is of course nothing but a poetical invention; but an invention, founded upon truth.

To be able to have emotions of sorrow and sadness, is a divine grace for him who became a sinner; and when necessary to *be able* to weep, is an outflow of divine compassion.

YET, and this should never be forgotten, with Jesus such emotion never became *passionate*. He did not give in to it. He sought no pleasure, in rousing it and giving ever stronger utterance to it. He did not willingly surrender Himself to it. Even then, when Jesus weeps, His sorrow is a weeping, marked by seriousness, and therefore by self-control. Not the crying of a child, but the silent, and therefore so significant, weeping of the Son of man.

Even in Gethsemane that dreadful perspiration shows, that Jesus did not surrender Himself, but kept up the struggle against the violent emotion, and His complaint to His disciples is a seeking of human help, not to sink away in the overwhelming power of the emotions.

Thus no cold impassiveness, however highly as *calmness* it may be advocated; but also no turning of emotion into wild *passionateness*.

Not the nerves, the *heart* must be touched in our emotions, and the pressure and impact of our nerves must be resisted, so soon as they would do anything else and anything more, than relieve the violently moved heart.

Jesus was *inwardly* moved, and that "inwardly" excludes the false play of nerves.

The nerves lie on the outside; the inward hides *in the soul.*

He who wants to affect the nerves, can make any one cry or laugh, without there being in the heart the least cause, that would move him to sadness or joy.

That play upon the nerves the children played in the streets of Jerusalem, and when it did not succeed, they complained: "We have played on the flute and ye have not danced, we have sung songs of mourning unto you and ye have not wept."

Even as in preaching also there was a time, when men sought to operate upon the *nerves* instead of upon the *soul.*

But with this the emotion, whereby Jesus was moved and stirred, has nothing in common.

Him wounded the sorrow *in the heart.* So He was *inwardly* moved. And it was that emotion of soul, that communicated itself to His flesh and finally took expression in the weeping of His eye.

Sensitiveness of heart therefore was the starting-point with Jesus. He felt so deeply and so tenderly.

Therefore has your Savior suffered all the days of His life, for all seeing of human sin and human misery gave Him inward *pain*.

And when, as in the betrayal, that *sin* was particularly strong in evidence, or when, as at Lazarus' grave, this misery showed itself in specially *shrill* colors, then it *shocked* Jesus, and then He became *inwardly* altogether moved, so that the emotion communicated itself to His entire being.


AND this is the way with the believer. Not so purely; not with that equipoise. With one more, with the other less. But yet the soul, that may believe, sometimes feels *pain*. Pain because of sin and pain at the sight of misery, sorrow and death.

Then something cuts within; not with an affected, but with a spontaneous bitterness. You feel, that there is a wound, and that with every emotion that wound smarts.

This is at one time by reason of one's own sins; then again because of the ruin worked by sin in your home, or in your environment of life, or brought about in God's Zion; or it is a human misery, which either overtakes you, or strikes you because others suffer.

Want and death are still so dreadfully abroad. There is so namelessly much suffered, that the shouts of merriment on the part of the world shall never hush the complaint of our misery.

On the deepest bottom of so many a soul there lies such nameless woe of heart.

The pessimist may feast himself on this woe, and the lover of pleasure may dismiss it with a laugh; he who is a child of God, and therefore understands something of the divine compassion, knows what it is, to be inwardly moved with compassion, and honors something *sacred*, something that may not be repressed, in his own sorrow and in that of others.

AND on this element of *sanctity* it depends.

In the work of nerves there is nothing sacred, and therefore you must not spare your nerves, but resist them medically and by way of chastisement.

But such is not the effect with him who is *inwardly moved*.

Then an anxious homesickness smarts within, springing up from a sacred remembrance, or sacred tie, that was broken, and still draws.

Amidst much work and diversion this temporarily passes away. But the wound remains. And no sooner is rest regained and remembrance awakened, but that pain within throbs again, and the emotion comes back.

And though in our busy life presently all sorts of things may divert us, or with new sorrow fresh emotion repress the old, yet the heart of God's child does not become unfaithful to its earlier sorrow. Only it sinks away in his heart a little more deeply, and is buried in one of those mysterious depths of his human

heart; until either already here remembrance wakes
it up again, or presently in our eternal existence the
fruit of all this "woe of heart" appears.


"Mixed with faith" remains therefore also with respect
to the world of our emotions the fixed stipulation.

For he who believes, can be so aboundingly happy
in it and thank his God for it, that he has once again
become aware of the tenderness of his own heart.

For it seemed sometimes many days, as though
everything within was frozen. So coldly and unsympa-
thetically you went along from day to day. Sometimes
it even gave you a feeling, as though you carried about
in your bosom a dead heart.

And see, now at once you discover, that this, God
be praised, is *not so*. Now you perceive, that when it
begins to storm in your life, and the wind blows off
the ashes from the seemingly extinguished coals of fire,
those coals are still possessed indeed of their former
glow. You then live at once so much more deeply, so
much more richly, so much more affectionately. Everything melts again. The wood of the trunk of your life
has become sappy again. You love so much more, and
it is as though indwelling sin no longer dares to show
itself at the windows of your heart.

And where in this way from such emotions faith
receives a beneficent impression, which leads to the
glorifying of God's name, that same faith puts the
bridle upon that emotion.

Also in deepest sorrow our Father in heaven may
not be denied; it may not seem to our soul, as though

there is no Reconcilor and Savior, as though there were no Comforter provided for our heart.

His love held the balsam in readiness, before He inflicted the wound.

And so by that love also *an emotion* must be quickened in our heart.

A being *moved* by the tendernesses of our God.

## XLIV

## "*A Judge of the Widows*"

### THE WIDOW

IN the state of widowhood there lies a thought of deep woe and crying homesickness.

At least if the previous life together in marriage, that was dissolved by death, even without being ideal, yet bore an ideal tint.

This is not said, as though there were no broad stream of domestic happiness and wealth of soul proceeding from marriage; but because more than anything else conjugal love has been pictured poetically, and thereby quickened in many a youthful heart ideals and illusions, which later on depress the reality of life.

For, truly, at times one finds a man and a woman, both of an equal highly-attuned spirit, whose married life seems to approach the ideal, and even the poetic ideal; but this is always an exception, and by far the greater part of marriages do not reach so far.

Actually thus the antithesis between happy and unhappy marriages lies somewhat lower; and one may prize the home already happy, where marriage grows and flourishes in personal attachment, in hearty sympathy, in oneness of faith and sense and spiritual direction, and where it is the mutual intent to make one another happy.

Already then married life bears an ideal tint.

And when death is sent to such a family, to take

the husband away, so that, with or without children, the wife remains behind, then that widow is the image of dismay and aching emptiness, which does not always crush, sometimes even lifts up the soul to God, but which always asks for support, and calls for comfort.

By the crying loss in so cutting a way the equipoise in her soul is broken; and all that is within her calls for something, by which that equipoise can be restored.

THEREFORE in His Word God comes to such a widow, and tells her, that He will be *a judge of the widows* (Ps. 68, 5).

It does not read, what many false readers have made of it, that God the Lord shall be the widows' *Husband.*

For that *thought* in Scripture there is even no room. The Lord is the Bridegroom of His *church,* to Israel an Husband, but for the desolate and bereft, the saddened and lonesome widow He is a *Judge,* even as to her orphans, that remain behind, He will be *a Father.*

That glorious promise therefore does not come, to draw to God the love of the woman's heart, that first went out to the husband. Even of such a transfer of love from the husband to God there can be no mention. Also before, also in marriage stood high and far, also above the love wherewith this widow cleaved to her husband, the love for God and her Savior; and where this was otherwise, it was not good.

Also to that widow so long as her husband lived, and not just now that he died, applied the high commandment that she should love God above all else, and her husband as herself. And to her also applied the word of Christ: "He who loveth husband or wife above Me, is not worthy of Me." If then there is a young woman, who in her first overwhelming love had forgotten God because of her husband, and had directed the first, the richest, the highest love of her heart to her husband instead of to her God, she fell into sin therewith, and she must seek atonement for this in the blood of the Lamb, and it may never be said, that her love for her husband was ideal, but rather with contrition and brokenness of soul it must be confessed, that her heart has led her astray.

WITH a widow therefore it makes such a deepgoing difference, not merely whether with the affectionate love of her heart, she has loved her husband, but especially also, whether with the highest love of her heart she has always loved her God, even above her husband.

Were this not so, then of course her distress is dreadful; for then, at least to her own sense of soul, with her husband she has lost everything; and then the first interest which at the grave of her husband she has to take in hand, is to convert herself to her God, and on His altar offer up to Him the so long withheld love of her heart.

With such widows in most cases during the first days you meet with certain despair, with passionate grief, in which speaks bitterness against her lot and a rebellious complaint against her God.

It storms then so bitterly in such a stricken heart. A God Who in His majesty draws near to comfort her, and Who can make no approach to her, except with a soul-wounding reproach. And in her troubled heart these two struggle in against each other. Now she will confess her guilt before her God, and again her heart inclines to break out in rebellion against God. And the sin of earlier days itself makes it impossible for the harmony, the peace, the eternal Sabbath to descend into her wild grief.

IT is altogether different, when a widow, also before she became a widow, has given her God a high place, her God even above all else, and has devoted to Him, her Father in the heavens, the first, the best, and holiest love of her womanly heart.

Then in her estimation it was always: God first, and *after that* my husband, as given me of God. Then it was every morning and every evening a giving thanks to God, for the rich possession for her heart she had received in her husband. And also, then it was, year after year, ever again a kneeling down together with that husband, to offer up to their God, in Whom the soul of each found her holiest point of union, the mingled offering of praise and love.

And, of course, when then the greatest distress of her life comes upon her, that God, Who gave her that husband, takes away again that husband from her side, then the loss is indeed unspeakable, and that transition truly dreadful, and that emptiness of her heart bitter to be borne; but yet for no moment can her heart grow rigid and cold, for it still kept all along the glow of its first and holiest love, i.e., the love for her God and her Lord.

A child, that in a troubled moment of his life still has his father with him, is altogether differently off, from a child, that must struggle through that same distress altogether forsaken.

And such is also here the antithesis.

A widow, who all the years of her married happiness continued to give God the first place in her heart, is, when the blow falls, indeed a child, that is cast into deep sorrow, but a child that in that sorrow still has her Father with her, can cast herself upon her God, and in the glow of that highest love of itself finds comfort with the grief, which by being cut off from her second love came upon the stricken heart.

You observe this, indeed, when you watch such a widow during the first days and weeks of her mourning.

For while the other one, who had given to her husband what was owing to God alone, bewildered and passionately cries and complains, you notice at once with a widow, who feared God and loved her God, what makes you say: No, that woman is *not* forsaken, she is *not* alone; and the love, that wells up from her heart, always yet possesses the highest object, toward which it went forth.

Thence that calmness in the sorrow, that peace amidst the terror of her heart, that plenitude of soul in the face of all that was taken from her. That restraint and self-control for what with the other became passionate and impetuous grief. Yonder something of the wildness, wherewith the lioness roars over her dead whelps, here the submissive surrender of a Christian woman, who enjoyed so deeply what the Lord gave and allowed her, but now also understands, that nothing, thus also not that tenderly loved husband, was her *property;* that everything belongs to God; and that she would not love her God to the full, if she placed her husband above Him, or if she wanted to keep that husband for herself, against the Lord's counsel.

BUT it is implied in the promise, that God will be a *Judge* unto her, and of this a tender-hearted widow has need.

She truly gave God always her first love, but in all earthly concerns she leaned upon her husband. She was subject unto him. He did everything. From him direction went out. She followed. She could not do otherwise. She had to do like this, otherwise she would have been no wife, and in her husband she would have had no real *husband.*

So God had ordained it. Such was with her the practice of faith also in her marriage. But now it cannot be otherwise, but that by the death of the husband, whom she so tenderly loved, and on whom she leaned so unconditionally, that *support* has fallen away from her.

She is now like ivy, that grew about the trunk of the oak. But see, that oak has been felled at the root, and the ivy lies on the ground.

And now her God will reveal Himself unto her in a new aspect of wealth. Inwardly He will raise her up and be Himself the trunk, to which the ivy can raise itself up again.

And this stands expressed in that forceful word, that God will be her Judge. For, of course, it is most trying to a widow, when, now that she is deprived of her husband, the outside world will take advantage of her weakness, by dishonorable dealings in the administration of her affairs.

This would render her helpless.

But no, then she does not stand helpless, for from heaven her God gives her the promise: *I will be your Judge.*

## XLV

## *"Sown in Corruption"*

### SOWN IN CORRUPTION

A MAN of great learning, who from the Synodical association had gone over to the church of Rome, recently entered the complaint, that among us, Protestants, the body of our dead was so carelessly handled.

He supposed that the separation of soul and body in dying was not yet entire, and that the separated soul therefore still needed some time, to withdraw itself altogether from the body, or to get away from the room and the house, where the body was; and that therefore it must be so painful to our dead, to have their body left alone in the dark, with no one to stay by, to pray and keep watch.

For this reason Rome's practices appealed to him. For in Romish families candles are burned by the side of the corpse, and family-members or else sisters of charity as a rule remain until burial, by day and by night, to keep watch over the corpse and to pray by its side.

Now let it be said at once, that this watching over a corpse is more a matter of luxury. When Protestant princes or princesses die, lights are kept burning in the same way by the side of the corpse, and in like manner the royal corpse is watched by night and by day; while on the other hand in poorer families also among the

Romish oftentimes little comes of this watching over the dead.

To a certain extent this splendid watching over a corpse is more closely related to the so-called *splendor ecclesiæ,* i.e., with the tendency in Rome's church, in every domain to appear with certain splendor.

Yet there is more in it than this.

The Romish representation expresses itself herein, that the transition from this life into blessedness is not at once consummated after death; but that after death a certain middle-state ensues, which is called purgatory; and that it is by the good offices of the church on earth, that the souls of the departed are delivered from purgatory.

Therefore Rome prays for her dead. Therefore she says masses for the dead. And therefore the relatives of the departed still offer all sorts of offerings and do good works, in the quiet confidence that these are to the good of the departed, and ameliorate their sufferings.

However touching this may seem, and whatever aftermath of love may express itself herein, it implies, that Rome thinks of her dead after death as *in a state of suffering,* from which only gradually they can be delivered, while we, with our fathers, confess, that he who dies blessed in the Lord, tastes *eternal joy* from his latest breath on.

And when you ask, what has the stronger appeal to the human heart, after death to be aware of much touching love in connection with the corpse, the whiles one is himself in purgatory, or immediately after dissolution to be with the Lord, then surely our Reformed confession with respect to this carries away the crown.

Blessed are the dead, who die in the Lord, from now on!

WITH this, however, all Protestant practice is by no means approved.

Not infrequently one has accustomed himself to a treatment of the corpse, which altogether antagonizes the claims of love and piety.

Then, as soon as death has entered, everything that is to be done is left to strangers. In times past these were neighbors; but now for the most part hired and paid persons. With these men there is no heart; and, by this constant care for the dead, human feeling is not infrequently hardened. What part strong drink plays in some places as a rule with this lugubrious business. And then, alas, the cases are not rare, that a corpse is made game of, and is treated in an irreverent manner.

And this must not be so. This is violation of the respect, which is due a corpse, because it is human. Herein speaks lack of awe in the presence of death. A brutality that wounds and offends.

Children of God will have nothing to do with veneration of a corpse. An exhibition of a corpse on a bed of state is offensive to them. Flowers and wreaths belong with the cradle and with the bridal gown, but never at the bier of the dead. That continual touch and kiss of the corpse is an expression of passion, which must be restrained, and held back.

Holy calm and quiet seriousness is the mood of mind and heart, suitable at the bier of our dead.

But that quiet, seriousness of mood will not tolerate injury, by what hurts or hinders the feeling.

And therefore with a corpse away with all exhibition of show, but also with a corpse *becoming reverence for the dead*.

GOD Himself appoints the moment, when you shall turn yourself away from the dead.

Immediately after death the corpse has something about it that attracts. And especially a few hours later, when our dead has been laid out, a corpse can be very beautiful, especially in contrast with the painful expression, that preceded dying. Only at the touch you feel, that the warmth of life has left, and the chill of death has followed, and that what lies before you, is not alive but dead. But for the rest you still seek the living person in it. It seems as though the face still speaks to you. And it would not seem strange, if the eye opened itself for a moment and the mouth would say a last farewell to you.

As long as this touchingly beautiful condition continues, God Himself in and by the corpse invites you, to prolong your tarrying with your dead. It does not repel as yet. It can still charm you. In holy quiet to gaze upon it, affects you beneficently.

There is then *no corruption yet*. And therefore you have no thought of burial yet; even if for no other reason, than to make sure, that you are not dealing with one only apparently dead.

That beautiful corpse is still dear to you.

But that does not last long. With sickness that

affected the blood, even but a very short time. And soon upon the pale marble of the corpse appear the blue, and presently the black-red spots. Dissolution goes on apace. What was shortly ago beautiful, becomes offensive and ghastly. Also the odor of death, that exhales from the corpse, tells you, that the corpse no more belongs to you, that it must be put away in the grave.

But . . . and with the touching parting from the corpse this is our boast and glory, we know, that, however deeply that corpse goes under in corruption and dissolution, it yet is *sown*.

It is no unsightly mass, that is cast away, to be rid of it. To bury is to sow in the acre of the dead. Confiding to the earth a self-dissolving corpse, that perishes, but in that corpse a germ, that is *sown*, that, when Christ comes back upon the clouds, at the resurrection of the flesh, that germ also will be made to unfold.

The soul of the departed, of course, does not suffer for a moment under this entrance upon corruption and that going down into the grave.

Our soul has an existence of her own, that in creation is bound to the body, and once shall go hand in hand again with a bodily existence; but the soul can be loosened by God from the body, as He once joined her to it; and as soon as death entered in and was consummated, whatever happens to the body, no more concerns the soul. Whether the corpses of our martyrs have been burned to ashes, or whether the corpses of our sailors have been devoured by sharks, the soul knows nothing of it. And God the Lord is able to watch over the germ of that corpse, altogether independent of whether the sea devours it or that fire consumes it. Also in that depth of the sea, and also in the crackling of the stake a *sowing* goes on.

Sown in *corruption* (I Cor, 15, 42) as every kernel of wheat must perish and must be unbound, that from it the blade might spring up; but yet in that corruptibility *sown*, so that from that wheatseed springs a new plant, and from that perished body of your dead proceeds once a new body.

THE soul of him who passes away, consummates her lot in dying itself.

For that soul everything depends upon the Mediator, the one and all forever on the Son of God.

If, before she separated from the body, one life's- and faith's-tie bound her to the Man of Sorrows, the King of glory, then death itself cuts off for her all fellowship with sin, and no valley of the shadow of death, and no Satan who wants to destroy us, can separate us from the love of Christ. Then she is unbound, to be forever with the Savior.

About the other case we prefer to maintain silence. It is so terrible. A soul that dies apart from Jesus. Nothing in all eternity binds her any more to the full-blessed Mediator. And no prayers or supplications on the part of those who remained behind can anymore save that soul from the eternal perdition.

Here, before dying, it must be decided forever.

But if he who dies, passed away in Jesus, be it

the child by yet unconscious grace, be it the adult by conscious faith, that had germinated from that grace, then that same Savior, Who has the soul in His keeping, watches also over your dust, that is confided to the earth, and you may commend the mortal remains of your dead to your Savior.

For what must perish in corruptibility, that it might be *sown,* shall once be raised in *incorruptibility.*

And that does not proceed as a process, that runs of itself. Also the kernel of wheat does not spring up of itself, but God brings up that wheatseed from its grave.

And so also it shall be here.

Flesh and blood cannot inherit the Kingdom of God, and so all that is corruptible in the corpse of your dead may freely perish, and, dissected in its parts, be absorbed by the earth.

Dust thou art, and to dust thou shalt return.

But what in that corpse constitutes *the germ* of the body, and hence is *sown* in that grave, that Christ shall once quicken.

Thus sounds the glorious word of promise, that by His apostle He has proclaimed to all the children of God:

"Who shall change our *humiliated* body, that it may be fashioned like unto his *glorious* body, according to the working, whereby he is able to subdue all things unto himself" (Phil. 3, 21).

## XLVI

# "In the Choice of Our Graves"

## OUR OWN GRAVE

AFTER dying comes burial.

You cannot truly say, that Holy Scripture counts burial lightly. You rather see all through Scripture, how strong the attachment was to an honorable, careful, stately burial. And when finally the grave opens itself for the body of your Savior, it affects the heart sweetly, that no rough soldier put Him away in the earth, but that men and women of influence tenderly care for the body of Jesus, swathe it, and carry it away, and place it in a new grave, and hold fragrant spices in readiness, and have bought balsam, in order, as soon as the Sabbath is over, to finish the burial of your Savior.

If ever it is at the funeral, at the carrying out of our dead to the grave that the human heart, the instinct of our human nature must be heard. The tie, that was cut off by death, must do its after-drawing. And in that very consecration and love, of which we give evidence for our dead, faith must forcibly express itself, that he who died is not gone, *but lives;* especially when we stand in the hope, that it is a life with God.

Therefore from of old there was something attractive in it, to do everything *ourselves,* and not *have it done* for money.

For money one can rid himself of everything. As soon then as your dead breathed his last, you summon the undertaker; you put him in charge of the corpse; then you are rid of everything; till the funeral procession is at the door, and you step into your carriage, to accompany the last rites.

But love does not do so, and in Christian Europe it used to be the rule in almost every way, that the care for the body remained altogether in the hands of the family, of friends or of neighbors.

Oneself to lay out the body, might have been too affecting sometimes for the wife, or for the husband; in which case the love of friend or neighbor supplied the needed help. Every one in the house did what he could, to care for the body, every time to go and look at it, and not to leave the mortal remains, till the hour of final separation.

WITH the sickly sentimentality, which is now abroad, to make everything of the corpse by way of adornment, this Scriptural, this Christian tenderness in the care for our dead has nothing in common.

Sentimentality is bent upon stimulating feeling; to bring the nerves into a state of tension; and in that pitiful excitement, that expresses itself in tears, to seek a sort of delight, or also to show openly, the warmth and devotion of our love.

This by itself has not the least merit. The issues of our life do not lie in our lachrymal glands, and equally little in our nerves, but in our heart. And he alone who can say, also when there is one dead in the home, that faith and love are active, that he might ask himself before God, how the Lord wills that we shall behave ourselves with respect to our dead, lives through those days of sorrow and of mourning according to God's Word.

And upon this holding of oneself to the ordinances of God emphasis must here be put.

The danger is not small, that in such days of sadness, when the blinds in the street are closed, one makes of his dead some sort of a half-idol, and forgets God the Lord.

You notice this in the conversations; then you see the homage that in many ways is paid to the corpse, especially with persons of high distinction; and then sometimes in so offensive a way you hear addresses at the grave, when he, whose breath was in his nostrils, and now died, is exalted as in a halo of glory, and every remembrance of the name of the Lord remains wanting.

FOR the most part one comes unexpectedly upon those days when "a corpse awaits burial." For even when dying has long been anticipated, one has but rarely placed himself in the condition that ensues, when the end has come.

In the first moments one is then overwhelmed with grief. Things must be done, and one does not know, how to do them. In the home, in the conversations, in the actions there is a general confusion. One is inclined to leave things to take care of themselves, and if then there is some one of the family, who offers to do things, he is given free hand to do as he thinks best.

So there is no operation of faith, no principle dominates. and in these latter times it is not infrequently the undertaker, who in every way decides for you, how your dead is to be buried.

And this is connected again with the pitiful sign of our times, i.e., that almost no one any more thinks of his death beforehand; that all familiarity with the idea of death is gone; and that one lets death overtake him, as a sandstorm a traveling caravan.

Of course, we do not mean, that every one personally should make it a point of honor, when there is one dead in his house, to make a show to the last particular, how well he understands the art of burying. That would be the pride of prudery; a soulless affectation which offends.

This evil was watched against even in former times, by ordering everything that pertained to burial, according to custom and as by mutual agreement.

At the grave no eccentricity was tolerated.

And so every region, and every city, and sometimes even every village had its own manners.

But in those manners there was seriousness, good taste was in evidence, a Christian view of Death and Grave; and it was from meditating and pondering upon Death and Grave among confessors of the Lord, that these funeral usages were born.

Now, on the other hand, all that meditating and pondering has ceased. Everything is left to itself. As a result of this, ancient usages are more and more transposed, now to become more and more dominated by the spirit of unbelief and deification of man, which holds sway in leading circles.

There is indeed something lovely about it, with one's fellow-citizens after death to be buried in the same cemetery; but Abraham thought differently about it.

Ephron offered him the communal grave for the body of Sarah; but Abraham wanted *a grave of his own* for his dead (Gen. 23).

And in this there is an indication for all who confess Christ, and in Christ the Victor over Death and the Grave.

A grave of one's own for the redeemed of the Lord will more and more seem an imperative need of our Christian life.

Otherwise Christendom itself will end with *heathen* burial.

THUS the main thing is, that from our *thoughtlessness* we come back again to *thoughtfulness.*

Therefore we wrote at the head of this meditation: "The *Choice* of Our Graves." He who has a choice, chooses, and he who chooses, has taken careful thought, and acts with self-consciousness, knowing what he is about.

And this is what is lacking in our days.

Now, when it comes to burying, no one takes thought. Everything is left to itself, or the usages of the world are imitated.

So altogether different from what it was with early Christians.

They at once abandoned mourning, they buried their dead in festal robes, and when the day was done, with torchlight, jubilantly singing psalms, they went to the cemetery, to testify before God and man, that this their brother or sister had passed over from the militant to the Church triumphant.

Their look upon Death and Grave was one altogether different from that of the heathen-world, and therefore also their usages at burial had to bear an altogether different character.

Death was to them a dying unto sin and an entrance into an eternal life.

Therefore with their dead they mourned little and jubilated much.

Something that is not said, that now also you should carry out your dead like this.

You must not imitate anything.

But what you should do, is, as they did, ponder yourself on Death and Grave, speak about Death and Grave, live as it were by anticipation through the experience of Death and Grave, and when the whole church of Jesus begins to do this, the good Christian manner of burial comes of itself.


THE mere expression of "the choice of our graves" stimulates thought, and strikes you in the conscience, as often as you have just left the burial of your dead to others, and have followed the usages of the world.

No glitter and vain shows have any place with your burials, to make others jealous. For exhibition of one's own greatness there is no worse occasion than when one of your own blood-relatives impotently is laid away in the grave.

Not selfishness, but love must urge and lead.

Love for him who went from you; always after this rule: As ye would, that others would do with you, when you have died, even so you yourself do unto your dead.

And, of course, with God's child that love must be directed not by sentiment, but by *faith*.

Wherever you could forget your God, you may never forget Him at the deathbed or at the grave of your dead.

Stronger than ever at every deathbed and at every opened grave the rule must hold good: *"In that day the Lord alone shall be exalted"* (Is. 2, 17).

## XLVII

## *"As the Angels of God"*

### THE SEEING AGAIN

THE wish, that one himself might die, is never more ardent in a man, than at the freshly dug grave of the dearest pledge, that he possessed on earth, and which God the Lord took from him.

If your love is divided among many interests, that urge speaks far less strongly; for to follow your dead in death, you would then have to part from what still remained to you. But when you are almost all alone in the world, and you were still so rich in your loneliness, because God had given you a tender wife or as woman a man after your own heart; or because as widow He had left you still an only child; and it happens that then that *only object of your love* is carried out, yea, then life renders you so mortally weary, and death exercises so wondrous an enchantment, that to die and to follow after your dead, seems bliss to the soul.

Nothing but death between you and the treasure of your love, that sank away in the grave.

O, do you not understand, that it has driven sometimes one shattered in mind to dreadful *guilty* suicide?

Through the depth of the waters back to him, whom she loved and could not miss.

And though with less passionate love this urge is less strong, and though in a rich possession, that still rested you, that urge finds a wholesome counterweight,

304

yet that deep longing *to see again, those who went from you,* is so general, so natural, so genuinely human, that, immediately after the dying, at least if there were any love, it almost always asserts itself.

YET do not attach *too much* to this.

Also your experience has taught, that this longing to see the departed again often seems more than it is.

Shortly after the dying; when all your nerves were tense; and death itself made the tie of blood and the tie of the heart speak most loudly; then, indeed, that longing after seeing again was real.

But let some three, four years pass by, and see what change already then has taken place. For the infant, that God took from you, He has given you other darlings in the place. For the life in the domestic circle, from which a brother or sister was removed by death, by marriage an entirely other life has come in place. How many a widow, who after three, four years already married again, and now devotes her love to another man, and presently to a new-born babe. And then in such a circle rouse for once the remembrances of the dead, and see, how altogether differently that longing after seeing again presents itself.

Not that therefore our dead are necessarily forgotten, or that a lack of reverence for their memory has entered in; and also not, that one would not willingly see him again. But yet the *longing* after it has then already become so much weaker. And that already after three, four years!

Let us therefore be sober, and always continue

mindful, that in the first days after the "dying" and "burial" our life is not normal, and all our life in an unnatural way is concentrated on one point.

There are indeed cases, where this is different.

When love for him whom God took from us was very deeply rooted; when God the Lord made almost everything sink away from us in that one grave; and when presently no change comes in our lot of life to break the bitter desolateness;—O, surely then it seemed, that longing after seeing again rather increased than diminished, and that after ten and twenty years the deep sighing of the soul ever yet went out to that one object of our love, that went from us and left us irrecoverably alone.

BUT also then such longing must stand under the discipline of God's Word . . . and God's Word has almost nothing to say about it.

If it had been the will of the Lord, that, after our death, we would have continued the old communal life with our early departed relatives or friends, Scripture would constantly have held this before you as allurement, to foster homesickness after the eternal fatherland.

But see, this God's Word does not do.

Scripture truly stimulates in you homesickness after the eternal fatherland, but never by rousing the longing in you after that seeing again, but solely by making you long *for your God and His blessed fellowship;* by infusing in you a longing of soul after your Savior; by making you thirst after the congregation of the elect; by making the inheritance of the saints in light glisten before you; and by pointing you to the day of glory, which comes with the Maranatha.

Recognition is thereby not excluded. The rich man in the parable recognizes Lazarus and Lazarus him; but when there is mention, of continuing the earthly relation between man and wife in the hereafter, Jesus rejects every such idea, by saying: "In heaven there is no marriage, but all God's saints are *as the angels of God*" (S. Matt. 22, 30). And you know, the love of God's angels goes out to the Lord of hosts and to that eternal Being alone.

And this is the tender point.

Also at the grave of your dearest dead you must ever be mindful of the high commandment, that your first, your deepest, your richest, yea, all your love must draw not to any one creature, but to Him, Who has made you.

Also at the grave of your dead God stands calling with holy jealousy: *"Give Me thine heart."*

And neither the bier, nor the grave, nor your overwhelming grief can take anything away from the holy ordinance, that you shall love the Lord your God with *all* your heart, with *all* your soul, with *all* your mind, and with *all* your powers.

And it is against this holy ordinance, that especially in days of bereavement sometimes so dreadfully, so thoughtlessly, and without any knowledge of sin, sin is committed.


AND yet, that holy jealousy of your God does not exclude therefore the human in the drawing of your heart, but merely demands that your grief shall not stand in the way of your love for your God.

What follows therefrom, you feel yourself.

Even this rule, that every tie, that was sanctified in God, remains, but also that every tie, that was apart from God, by death is loosed forever.

If your child, that God took from you, was nothing to you but a doll to play with, your delight and your enchantment; if there was nothing else and nothing deeper back of your love; if there was no tie in Baptism, no tie in the Covenant, no tie in prayer, no tie that bound you with your child to your God, confess, what then in that eternal life would there be in common between you and your darling?

And as it is with your child, so it is with all your dead. You may have felt yourself, O, so much interested by so much; by so much that was lovely in the external, by so much that was delightful in life, by so much that was friendly and captivating; under the cherishing of all this loveableness you may, as it were, have been welded together, so that your life was interbraided with the life of your dead; and yet, if there operated no higher fellowship in the worship of your God and in the love for your Savior, what then will there ripen from so earthly an inclination for or bloom after among the angels of God?

Surely, there is a resurrection of the flesh, and however glorious the garments of light shall be, in which God's saints shall dwell on the new earth under the new heaven, there shall be resemblance, and recognition of those whom we have known on earth is not excluded. But you also know, if you come where Lazarus awoke, you can only have fellowship with those who awake where you are. From all others a chasm separates you, which no one can bridge over.

God's children alone come thus with God's children together; and they come together without sin, in a state of spiritual perfection, in which the love of all for the Eternal Being shall be perfect.

How then in such a heavenly state would a love, that did not root in God and operated apart from the tie to God, be possible, or also even be thinkable?

AND now you feel the power, that goes out from this exalted viewpoint.

For, there follows from it, that already here on earth you have to see to it, that every tie with husband or wife, of father or mother, of child or friend is not left outside of your love for God.

A heart, that is still divided, is powerless.

And so long as you still have your love for your God on one hand, and on the other an entirely different love for your relatives and friends, there lacks in you that inner harmony, wherein lies the beauty of the soul.

That avenges itself at dying, and not infrequently at the grave you will wage a bitter fight between your love for your God and the love for your dead, and often the passion in your grief pushes then your love for your God into the background.

But if it became different, and your fellowship with your wife and with your child became more and more a fellowship in Christ, a fellowship founded in the love for your God, then that breach does not come, and also at the grave of one most tenderly loved the

*Soli Deo gloria,* in which the greatest part of your heart sank away, is not denied.

Then also at your graves the love for your God continues to excel all else, and when you think of eternity and of your own dying, you do not think first of the seeing again of your dead, but before everything else of the seeing of your Savior and of the vision of your God; and then it is from His love, that you expect back again that fellowship alone with your dead, that can glorify Him and is granted you by His grace.

## XLVIII

## *"To Be Clothed Upon"*

### TO BE CLOTHED UPON

Wʜᴇɴ we stand at the bier of our dead, the church of Christ puts upon our lips the mysterious confession: "I believe in the resurrection of the flesh." And from this point, every representation must start out, which we form of the lot and the condition of our dead.

It does not avail you, that you say to yourself, that you have to leave with the Lord the lot of your dead. This will do with one dead, who leaves you indifferent. But it does not do, when by the dying of one of your loved ones you were deeply wounded in your heart, and when his image still rises every time before you, to interest you and keep you engaged and to overtake you with that multitude of questions, that with the mystery of death presses upon you.

This is so true, that also the nations, which by reason of their sins have been given over by God to a reprobate mind, yet could not rest, until, in however imperfect a way, they had discovered some answer to those questions. And it is only the unbelievers of our nineteenth century, who at the grave of their dead impose silence upon all thought; hide the casket under wreaths of flowers; and scarcely dare to mention still a *hope* of immortality.

In the end cremation of the body is yet most fully in harmony with their nihilistic somberness.

But so it is not with God's child in the cemetery.

To him a light is risen in this darkness of the grave. And in that light Christ's church does not leave him perplexed, but gives him so much assurance in his representation, that, in thinking of his dead, his heart is no playball of anxiety and uncertainty, but comes at length to rest.

"WE know," so spake the holy apostle, "that, if our earthly house of this tabernacle were dissolved, we have a building of God, an house not made with hands, eternal in the heavens" (II Cor. 5, 1).

And you know what in their mutual antithesis "Tabernacle" and "House" indicate.

Moses first built a "Tabernacle" which was adapted, to serve on the pilgrim-journey through the wilderness. And afterward Solomon built the Lord an "House," on that Zion, which He had chosen as a place of His rest.

Beautiful and striking thus is the apostolic comparison.

Our body, in which we continue our pilgrim-journey to the grave, is merely our *tabernacle*, which is destined once to be dissolved and to disappear like the tabernacle, Moses built. But when that tabernacle of this earthly body is dissolved, there comes afterward for that tabernacle a fixed "building," an "house," a real "dwellingplace" in its stead, that shall very far excel the tabernacle in splendor and glory.

He who looked attentively upon Solomon's temple, saw in that temple the tabernacle. The same thought lay expressed therein; it was built after the same division of ground; the same fundamental lines were traced therein. And yet that temple was so altogether different. Everything fixed what in the tabernacle was loose. The finishings were far richer. The form far more ornamental. The splendor far more brilliant.

You could say: In the tabernacle lay the germ of the temple; and again in the temple the tabernacle was gloriously risen.

And by the mouth of the apostle, the Holy Spirit applies this to the mortal remains of your dead.

Also that provisional body, in which you have known them, even as the tabernacle, attracted you by charms of many sorts; but it was weak in its articulations, it remained frail and transitory. Once it had to be dissolved, and as afterward in Israel you heard nothing more of the tabernacle, so also that earthly body of your child, of your wife, of your husband, of your brother, of your sister had *quietly to perish.*

But because the tabernacle disappears, every form of the sanctuary of Israel does not pass away.

On the contrary, in the breaking down of the tabernacle lies the prophecy of the temple that is to come. And so also in that dying, in that breaking down of the body of your dead, lies for you the glorious prophecy of a far more glorious form, in which once they shall arise.

For, also when their body of this earthly tabernacle is dissolved, God's Word says to you: This your dead, provided he departed in life-fellowship with Christ Jesus, shall have a *building* of God, an *house,* not made with hands, and shall once be clothed upon with his "habitation" from the heavens.

Solomon built his temple not from the several parts of the tabernacle, and so also that flesh and blood, that goes into dissolution in the grave, shall not inherit the Kingdom of heaven. And yet tabernacle and temple are one, even as the blade is one with the kernel of wheat from which it sprang. It is the same fundamental trait. From the tabernacle the temple has come forth. But what was brittle wood in the tabernacle is hewn stone in the temple. And in the temple there was a ceiling covered with gold for what were skins over the tabernacle. Not something different, it is the same, and yet different, because so much more glorious.

Think how S. John on Patmos saw the Savior. Ever yet the same Who was born in the crib of Bethlehem, but now shining in majesty, His eyes as a flame of fire, His hair like unto white wool, His feet glowing as shining brass, and His voice as the sound of many waters. The same and yet an altogether different body. Now in splendor and glory. And it is like unto this His glorified body, that once He shall make the body of your dead; if indeed they are of His, adopted in the fold of that One and Only Shepherd.

Thus you have firm ground under foot.

Before everything else the main question, whether he who went from you, was incorporated in the mystical body of Christ. If this were so, then likewise the full assurance, that now the "tabernacle of this earthly body" is truly broken down, but that your beloved dead shall one day obtain back a far more glorious form. For that frail tabernacle a glorious temple. A new and glorious body, that shall be a temple of God in the Spirit. An habitation eternal in the heavens. A heavenly and pure form, always according to the fundamental traits and fundamental division of the body that here went under, but then no more subjected to corruption. As the apostle says: *an house of God.*

ONLY, for this you also know, *so it is not yet.*

All this tarries and bides till the sign of the Son of man shall be seen upon the clouds. For, then only shall your dead arise, and you with them.

Until that illustrious day your dead are what in II Cor. 5, 3, the holy apostle calls "unclothed" or "naked"; that is to say, that they exist only in their soul, as spirits, and, for a time deprived of all external appearance, they lack the possession of the body.

They have their tabernacle *no more,* and their temple they have *not yet.*

Just as for a time the ark of the Covenant stood on Zion, while there was no more tabernacle, and the temple had not yet been built.

Something that certainly sounds very strangely to the wise of this age, who have told you, that soul and body cannot possibly be two substances, but a fact, that has nothing in the least problematical about it for him who knows, that God in Paradise first formed Adam's body, and then in that body increated the soul.

It is indeed noteworthy, therefore, that later philosophers already now again incline to similar representations. Herbart, the philosopher who exerts so great an influence, already preached something, that comes much closer to what God revealed unto us.

But whatever the wise men of this age may cogitate and ponder, we *know,* that there is a God Who lives,

Who can destroy both *body and soul* in hell, but also a God, Who can take up, both body and soul into His glory.

As now God's angels *always* exist without body, so also your dead, because they have a soul, can exist for a time as spirits, without body. Only with this difference, that an angel without body is *not* "naked" and *not* "unclothed," because a body does not belong with him. But that your beloved dead, on the other hand, in that separated spiritual state of soul, are indeed "naked" and truly "unclothed," because they lack their corruptible body, and have not yet received from God their eternal body.

Thus they are *blessed*.

For they have died unto all sin. All their tears have been wiped away. Nothing separates them longer from the blessed fellowship of their Savior. And they share the joy of their God.

Only, they are not yet *glorified*.

Therefore it is said in Revelation, that there are blessed ones who cry: "How long yet, O holy and righteous Ruler!" and that they are told, that they must yet wait awhile.

Therefore not only *love*, but also *hope* went with them across Death and Grave into eternity. For also their outlook and their blessed expectation is ever directed to that illustrious day, when God Triune shall forever triumph over Satan and all the power of darkness, and nothing more shall resist the glory of Christ, their King.

Then also they shall be "clothed upon." They simultaneously with you, provided it is also granted you, blessedly to die in your Savior. They shall not come in in advance of you, and you shall not come in in advance of them. But it shall be in one moment of time, with one sound of the trumpet, that every soul, that is reconciled in Jesus, shall receive their glorious body, then after soul and body eternally to live unto God.

**THE END**